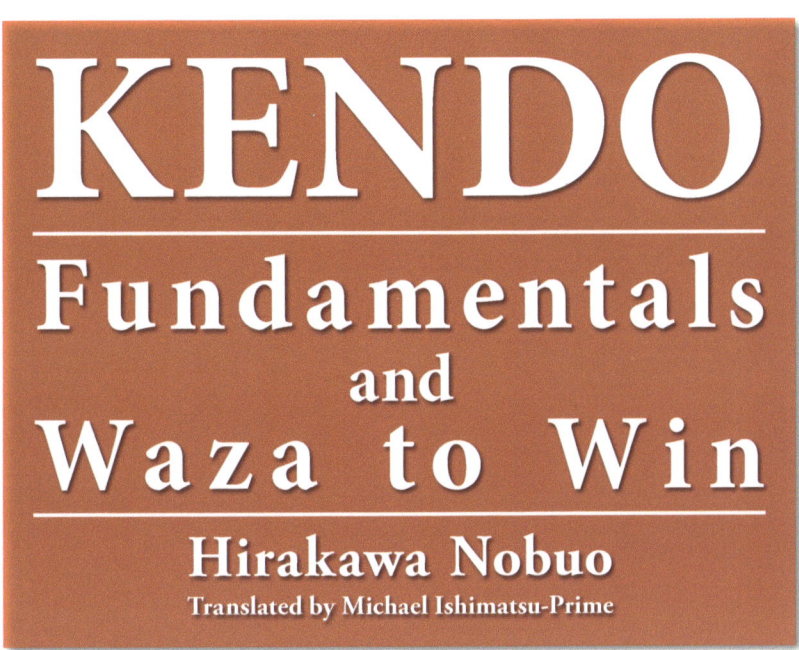

Credits

Translated by Michael Ishimatsu-Prime

Editing and Proofreading by Alex Bennett, Trevor Jones, Bryan Peterson, Yulin Zhaung

Photography by Shishikura "Kan" Masashi

Layout and Design by Baptiste Tavernier, Shishikura "Kan" Masashi

© 2019 Bunkasha International Corp.

Chiba, Japan

ISBN 978-4-907009-26-7

Contents

Foreword 1

The Concept of Kendo & The Purpose of Practicing Kendo 2

Chapter 1: The Outline of Kendo
    Kendo—Its History and Current State 3
    Kendo's Characteristics 4
    Types of Kendo Keiko 5

Chapter 2: Basic Skills
    Section 1: Correct Posture and Bowing
        1. *Shizentai*—natural posture 7
        2. *Rei*—courtesy and etiqutte, bowing 7
        3. *Kamae* and *osame*—*en garde* and sheathing the *shinai* 8
        4. *Ashi-sabaki*—footwork 12
        5. *Suburi*—how to swing the *shinai* 13
        6. How to wear *bogu*—protective armour 16
        7. How to store *bogu* 20
    Section 2: Basic Strikes (*uchi*) and Thrusts (*tsuki*)
        1. How to strike *men* 21
        2. How to strike *kote* 22
        3. How to strike *doh* 24
        4. How to *tsuki* 24
    Section 3: Basic Defence
        1. Defending against a *men* strike 26
        2. Defending against a right-*kote* strike 27
        3. Defending against a right-*doh* strike 27
        4. Defending against *tsuki* 28
    Section 4: *Kirikaeshi* (*uchikaeshi*)
        1. How to perform *kirikaeshi* (*uchikaeshi*) 29
        2. How to receive *kirikaeshi* 31
        3. Applied practice 32

Chapter 3: Applied Techniques
  Section 1: *Shikake-waza*
   1. Creating an opening with the *shinai* tip ········ 35
   2. Creating openings through body movement ········ 43
   3. Creating a *debana* striking opportunity ········ 50
   4. Creating an opening by suppressing the opponent's *shinai* and taking the centreline ········ 53
   5. Creating an opening with *ni / san-dan renzoku-waza* (continuous strikes) ········ 64
   6. *Taiatari-waza*—body-checking ········ 92
   7. *Tsubazeri-waza (hiki-waza)* ········ 96
   8. *Katsugi-waza* ········ 102
   9. *Katate-waza*—one-handed techniques ········ 104
   10. *Tobikomi-waza* ········ 111

  Section 2: *Kaeshi-waza*
   1. *Nuki-waza* ········ 112
   2. *Amashi-waza* ········ 116
   3. *Uchiotoshi-waza* ········ 117
   4. *Suriage-waza* ········ 121
   5. *Harai-waza* ········ 125
   6. *Osae-waza* ········ 129
   7. *Hari-waza* ········ 132
   8. *Maki-waza* ········ 136
   9. *Oji-kaeshi-waza* ········ 140

  Section 3: *Jodan-waza*
   1. *Katate-waza* ········ 146
   2. *Morote-waza* ········ 148
   3. *Waza* for use against *jodan* opponents ········ 149

Chapter 4: *Kata* ········ 151

Foreword

Kendo—the Way of the Sword—originates in Japan, and is the product of centuries of historical change. It is a unique and traditional form of athletic culture, but it is more than just physical exercise. Kendo is also a means of self-cultivation with the potential to be a positive spiritual and moral guide for practitioners. It has been adopted as part of the Japanese school curriculum because of its recognised educational value.

Today, kendo is not only practised in Japan by millions of men and women of all ages, it is also spreading throughout the world with the number of serious kendo practitioners outside Japan increasing. However, a recent trend has seen more people place importance on the competitive side of kendo rather than value it as a "Way" of spiritual or mental training.

There is no retirement in kendo. To enjoy it over a lifetime, as many practitioners do, it is essential to learn the fundamentals properly. This is the quickest way to become proficient. Once a good understanding of the basics has been attained, then one can set about mastering the advanced techniques. In this book, I use photographs to explain kendo's many techniques—from the basics through to applied techniques.

An ancient proverb states, "One sword becomes ten-thousand; ten-thousand swords return to one." Whatever your age, have fun studying and practising kendo's various techniques, and try to acquire one technique that you can win with every time. Alongside perfecting techniques, the kendoka aims to forge their mental, technical and physical strength, as this will have a positive impact in day-to-day life. To this end, this book aims to help you to learn the correct way of doing kendo.

Finally, I would like to thank the following people who helped to make the original Japanese version of this book possible when it was published in 1993: Kamei Toru (Hanshi 8-dan), Tominaga Takao (Kyoshi 7-dan), and Otake Kunihiro from Baseball Magazine Company. I would also like to thank Alex Bennett, Michael Ishimatsu-Prime, Shishikura Masashi, and Baptiste Tavernier of Bunkasha International for preparing the English language translation of this book, and to Miya Katsuyuki of Kodansha Ltd. for the use of Noma Dojo.

The Concept of Kendo

The concept of Kendo is to discipline the human character through the application of the principles of the Katana (sword).

The Purpose of Practicing Kendo

The purpose of practicing Kendo is:
To mold the mind and body,
To cultivate a vigorous spirit,
And through correct and rigid training,
To strive for improvement in the art of Kendo,
To hold in esteem human courtesy and honour,
To associate with others with sincerity,
And to forever pursue the cultivation of oneself.
This will make one be able:
To love his/her country and society,
To contribute to the development of culture
And to promote peace and prosperity among all peoples.

Chapter 1
The Outline of Kendo

Kendo—Its History and Current State

Of all the different weapons it is the sword that has been held in high esteem since antiquity in Japan with many myths and legends associated with it. Because the sword is one of the "Three Imperial Regalia", the other two being a mirror and a jewel, they are apotheosised as sacred objects in many Shinto shrines. Swords were awarded to warriors by the Shogun (the military rulers of Japan) on the occasion of new appointments, which is testament to their symbolism for political power. In this sense, the sword was not just a weapon to be used in conflict, it also represented social order and peace, and was respected by the Japanese people as a whole.

The manufacture of swords was originally influenced by China. Early swords were usually straight and flat. A new Japanese style of sword with *shinogi* ridges on each side, and curved single-edged blades was forged in Japan from the 10th century. Called *tachi*, swordsmanship was then referred to as "*tachikaki*" or "*tachiuchi*". From around this time, Japan became increasingly unstable, and to defend their territories, retainers of landowners specialised in the martial arts and earned honourable reputations through military prowess. This was the beginning of the samurai.

As samurai culture evolved, so too did the manner in which the sword was used. Through experience borne of actual combat, a distinctive Japanese style of sword usage was devised, and this would become the basis for kendo today. With the onset of the Kamakura period (1185-1333), the samurai established a new political centre in Kamakura, and the warrior class ruled Japan from then until the Meiji Restoration of 1868. Swords were always considered an indispensable weapon in the warrior arsenal, but the bow and arrow was their primary tool of war during the Kamakura era.

In the latter part of the Muromachi period (1333–1573), Japan entered an era of civil war known as the Warring States period. It was around this time that distinctive schools of swordsmanship known collectively as *ryuha* evolved. By the Tokugawa period (1603-1868), it is estimated that over 700 *ryuha* for swordsmanship existed, many of which stemmed from three prototypical schools from the Warring States period: Shinto-ryu, Kage-ryu, and the Chujo-ryu. Protective armour and *shinai* (bamboo swords) were devised by Naganuma Shirozaemon of the Jikishinkage-ryu and Nakanishi Chuzo from the Itto-ryu in the eighteenth century. Until that time, set forms practised with a partner using wooden or live blades known as *kata* were the standard method for learning and transmitting the school's techniques. With the invention of the *shinai*, however, swordsmanship took on a new dimension through safe full-contact sparring.

During the Meiji period (1868–1912), the policy of national seclusion which had prohibited contact with the outside world was abolished. An influx of Western ideas followed, and traditional Japanese culture went into decline. Class distinctions were abolished, and the samurai existed no more as a social entity. Kendo was in danger of becoming extinct, especially after the 1876 edict that forbade the carrying of swords in public. In 1879, however, the national police force adopted kendo training as a way to keep its constabulary fit and ready for duty. Kendo flourished in the police, and gradually established a new niche in the modern era.

In 1895, the Dai Nippon Butokukai (Greater Japan Martial Virtue Society) was established as the gatekeeper for traditional martial arts, and kendo gained an enthusiastic following among members of the public. In 1911 kendo and judo were permitted as official subjects for physical education in middle and normal schools. In 1912, the first year of the Taisho period (1912-1926), representative techniques from various *ryuha* were adapted to formulate the Nippon Kendo Kata for the promotion of a standardised style of kendo nationwide.

Such was the prestige attached to the martial arts that tournaments were held before the emperor in 1929 for the coronation of Hirohito, in 1934 to celebrate the birth of the crown prince, and in 1940 to mark 2600 years of imperial rule in Japan. These were the golden years for modern kendo. Kendo eventually became a compulsory subject in Japan's schools during the militaristic 1930s and '40s, and following Japan's defeat in World War II, kendo and other martial arts were completely prohibited in schools and the community following the dissolution of the Dai Nippon Butokukai. Once again kendo looked as though it might disappear completely.

In 1950, the All Japan Shinai Sports (*shinai-kyogi*) Federation was inaugurated, following the creation of a hybrid form of kendo that resembled Western fencing. In 1952, *shinai-kyogi* was permitted in schools but with the signing of the San Francisco Peace Treaty in 1952, the All Japan Kendo Federation (AJKF) was launched and kendo proper was resurrected in schools from 1953. *Shinai-kyogi* and kendo merged in 1954 to make "school kendo", and the All Japan Shinai Sports Federation was absorbed into the AJKF. In 1955, the AJKF became an affiliate of the Japan Athletic Association meaning that kendo could participate in the 10th National Sports Meet as an official event.

Since its inauguration, the AJKF has been active in the promotion of kendo as a modern sport suited to the needs of contemporary society. The AJKF developed protocols for how competitions would be conducted, match rules, titles and grades. The AJKF is also responsible for holding important events such as the annual All Japan Kendo Championships, All Japan East vs. West Championships, the All Japan Prefectural Championships, and so on.

The International Kendo Federation (FIK) was launched in 1970. At the time of publication (2019), there are 57 countries and regions registered with the FIK, and around another 50 that practise kendo. The FIK also organises the World Kendo Championships (WKC) every three years. The 16th WKC was held in May 2015 at the Nippon Budokan, in Tokyo, Japan, and the 17th WKC was held in Incheon, South Korea, in September 2018. Both of these WKC had 56 countries and over 800 participants and officials taking part. The 18th WKC will be held in Paris, France, in 2021.

Traditionally, kendo was taught mainly to boys, and the art of naginata (halberd) to girls. In the post-war period, however, women kendoka have continued to increase. In 1962, the first All Japan Women's Kendo Championship was held, and the following year girls competed at the All Japan High School Sports Federation kendo event alongside the boys. 1984 saw the first National Housewives Kendo Competition take place, and a women's competition was officially established at the World Kendo Championships in 2003. Kendo is truly for everyone, everywhere.

Kendo's Characteristics

Kendoka wear *kendo-gi* (thick cotton top) and *hakama* (pleated split-skirt). For armour, there is the *men* (a head protector), *kote* (hand and forearm protectors), *doh* (torso protector), and *tare* (waist, lower abdominal and hip protector). Representing the sword is the *shinai* made from four slats of bamboo strapped together with leather fittings.

Etiquette is emphasised in kendo. It is deemed important to respect the opponent and to maintain correct posture and *kamae* (stance) of the mind and body. Matches take place on wooden-floored square courts that measure between 9 and 11 metres each side. Competitors vie to take the best of three *yuko-datotsu*—a valid strike or thrust. There are individual and team bouts, and "winner-stays-on" team matches. The winning team is decided by the aggregate number of wins. If this is equal, victory is determined by the most points scored. Matches are usually five minutes or less in duration. In the case of individual competitions, extra-time (*encho*) may be utilised in a sudden-death decider if the result is not decided within the allotted time. Matches are officiated by three referees - one chief referee and two sub-referees.

In the All Japan Kendo Federation's "Concept of Kendo", it states that, "*The concept of Kendo is to discipline the human character through the application of the principles of the Katana (sword).*" Kendo is therefore an educational vehicle that aims for the perfection of character. Accordingly, as it meets criteria set by the Japanese Ministry of Education, Science and Culture, it has been adopted as a subject in physical education classes at both junior and senior high schools.

For a strike to be judged as valid (*yuko-datotsu*), it must be made with full vigour, correct posture, and with the top quarter of the *shinai* (*datotsu-bu*) accurately striking the target. It is also necessary to strike from the correct distance (*maai*), with a unification of spirit, sword, and body. A successful attack must also be followed by a demonstration of continued physical and psychological alertness (*zanshin*). Simply put, these are all the requirements to score a point in kendo. It is not just a matter of hitting the opponent randomly.

Kendo fosters correct posture, explosive power, agility, skill, and stamina. From a mental and social perspective, kendo encourages courtesy, respect for one's opponent, an independent spirit, energy, decisiveness, and concentration. Regardless of age or gender, kendo can be adjusted to suit your physical condition, making it possible to compete into old-age.

Types of Kendo Keiko

After attaining a degree of proficiency in basic movements, *uchikomi-kirikaeshi*, and applied techniques (*shikake-waza* and *kaeshi-waza*), they must be continually practised so that they can be used freely against opponents. This is "*keiko*".

The word "*keiko*" consists of two *kanji*: "*kei*" (稽) means "to think" or "to consider", and "*ko*" (古) means "old" or "ancient". "*Keiko*" therefore means "to consider the past", or "train while reflecting upon the teachings of ancients".

There are many different types of *keiko*, each with its own purpose and methods. *Keiko* can be classified into the following types: *kihon-geiko* (basics practice); *uchikomi-geiko* (striking practice); *kakari-geiko* (attack practice); *hikitate-geiko* (sparring in which the senior encourages or guides a lower level practitioner); and *shiai-geiko* (match or competition practice). There are also some special types such as *kan-geiko* (mid-winter training), *shochu-geiko* (mid-summer training), *ensei-geiko* or *musha-shugyo* (travelling around to train), and *tachikiri-geiko* (a special event where one person will fight up to 33 people in succession without a break).

1. *Kihon-geiko*

In *kihon-geiko* it is essential that the practitioner first makes a strong base. This consists of good posture, *kamae*, footwork, and the ability to swing the *shinai* properly. From there, the practitioner can strike an imaginary opponent, an *uchikomi-bo* (a stick or *shinai* held by the instructor), or a practice dummy. However, to completely learn the basic strikes, more than anything you will need to repeatedly practise with an actual opponent.

Kage-uchi-keiko (shadow striking) is done alone against an imaginary opponent to work out your own thoughts on kendo. As you learn the techniques and body movements, your bad habits will become apparent and can be rectified. It is also possible to study someone's strong points, and learn correct basics and technique from watching their *keiko*. This is known as *mitori-geiko* (practice through observation).

2. *Uchikomi-geiko*

In *uchikomi-geiko* the instructor or *motodachi* creates openings which must be struck immediately with a stable posture and energy. The main point of this exercise is to learn basic strikes, to be able to move the body quickly, and to develop stamina. *Uchikomi-geiko* must be done with big, correct strikes. A variation is "*uchikomi-kirikaeshi*"—striking centremen, followed by *renzoku-waza*, and then *tai-atari*, and finished with *kirikaeshi*.

3. Kakari-geiko

The purpose of *kakari-geiko* is to become proficient at *shikake-waza*. You continuously and vigourously attack a *motodachi* or instructor for a short period of time, with absolute conviction, using all the skills that you have at your disposal. It is important to make big strikes with the whole body. The *motodachi* may deflect incorrect or half-hearted strikes, or when they are lacking in spirit, by attacking back or doing *tai-atari*. *Kakari-geiko* develops a robust body and spirit along with making the practitioner's body movements free and nimble.

4. Hikitate-geiko

Hikitate-geiko is the opposite of *kakari-geiko*. It is sparring in which the instructor or high-ranked *motodachi* encourages the lower-ranked practitioner, allowing them to strike freely. When the *motodachi* sees an opening, they too will strike to make the opponent aware of their mistake. The *motodachi* must move vigorously and make the opponent maintain and attack from the correct *maai*. Furthermore, it is important that *motodachi* makes the opponent understand opportunities to strike.

5. Gokaku-geiko

Gokaku-geiko (also called *ji-geiko*) is sparring practice against someone who is of equal skill. From the correct *maai*, look for good opportunities and attack with a strong spirit. Even though your opponent might be stronger, do not be afraid. If they are weaker, treat them as an equal, not an inferior. It is important to put everything into getting the first strike, to compete fair and square, and with a good fighting spirit. *Gokaku-geiko* is important for perfecting your own *waza*, and you should to strive to master advanced techniques.

6. Shiai-geiko

Shiai-geiko (match practice) is done before competitions to create the type of atmosphere that you would experience in a tournament. With somebody standing in as referee, you can have your basics and techniques evaluated objectively. You can also learn how to referee, and understand the good and bad points of the competitors you are adjudicating.

While competitions are something that you should train seriously for, do not forget that they are not the be-all and end-all aim of kendo. A distinction should not be made between regular practice and competitions: practise both with the same mindset. In a competition, you can learn the effectiveness of your techniques and become aware of matters that need further reflection. You must then make every effort to improve the quality of your *ippon*.

> **"Sanma no kurai"—The Three Attitudes to Polish Your Kendo**
>
> There are three important factors in the study of kendo: learn from a good teacher; make good friends, and encourage each other in *keiko*; be constantly inventive and creative. These factors are integral to one's development and are known as "the three attitudes to polish your kendo".

Chapter 2
Basic Skills

SECTION 1
Correct Posture and Bowing

1. *Shizentai*—natural posture

Shizentai forms the basis of *kamae*—a stance or posture from which one is able to defend or attack. Standing in *shizentai* means that the whole body must be well balanced, stable, and free of tension. It will then be possible to move the body to defend or attack with complete control. Being a natural standing position, *shizentai* can be maintained for a long time and help foster a good posture in one's daily life.

Straighten your back, then take a deep breath and hold it in the lower abdomen. The heels are placed together gently on the ground as if they are floating. Relax both shoulders, extend the neck, and pull the chin in. Put pressure in the toes and straighten the legs with the feeling of pushing your centre of gravity forward. The eyes are kept wide open.

Shizentai **(front & side)**

2. *Rei*—courtesy and etiquette, bowing

Kendo involves vigorous striking, thrusting, and counterattacking. Consequently, practitioners can become overly excited in the fray, which is why it is important to show mutual respect. It is said that in order to cultivate one's self in kendo, one must "Start with *rei*, and finish with *rei*." For that reason, a great deal of importance is attached to the idea of *rei* and protocols of etiquette.

How to sit and stand

From *shizentai*, sit down by bending the left knee first and then the right. Cross both the big toes, open the knees to approximately the width of two fists, straighten the back, tense the lower abdomen, and rest both hands lightly on the upper thighs. The shoulders are free of tension and the chin is pulled in with the mouth closed. Look straight ahead.

Do in reverse when standing up. (Start by extending the right leg and then the left.)

Sit from the left leg

Seiza **(seated posture)**

Stand from the right leg

7

Zarei—seated bow

From *seiza*, look at the opponent and prostrate the upper body forward. Slide both hands in front of the knees making a triangle shape on the floor with the forefingers and thumbs. Calmly lower the head, and return to the original position after one breath.

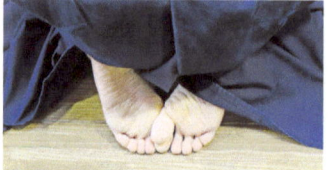
Cross both big toes

Seiza (side)

Seiza

Place both hands in front

Lower the upper body

Ritsurei—standing bow

Look at the opponent from *shizentai*. Hold onto the *shinai* lightly with the left hand near the *tsuba* (guard) with the *tsuru* (the cord holding the *shinai* together) facing down. Then bend the upper body forward about 20° with the hands hanging naturally by the sides. Take one breath and return to the original position. Place your thumb on the *tsuba* and grip the *shinai* at your left hip in the *taito* posture.

Sageto   ***Ritsurei***   ***Taito***   ***Sageto*** (side)   ***Ritsurei*** (side)   ***Taito*** (side)

3. *Kamae* and *osame*—*en garde* and sheathing the *shinai*

From the *taito* position with the *shinai* held at the left hip, move the right leg slightly forward while taking hold of the *tsuka* (the hilt) near the *tsuba* from underneath with the right hand. "Unsheathe" the *shinai* in a diagonal upward motion. Then, take hold of the *tsukagashira* (the end of the hilt) with the left hand while crouching down into *sonkyo* (squatting position). Stand up while moving the right foot forward slightly to assume *chudan-no-kamae* (middle stance).

To sheathe the *shinai* (*osame*) from *chudan-no-kamae*, point the toes of both feet slightly out and crouch down into *sonkyo*. When performing *osame*, place the *shinai* on the left hip and stand up as you release the right hand. Move the right foot back to assume the *taito* posture and then bow.

Kamae and *osame*

1. Proceed to the starting point and perform *ritsurei* from the *sageto* position
2. Assume the *taito* position and move three steps forward
3. Proceed to the start line and draw the *shinai* without touching the tip
4. *Sonkyo*
5. After the proclamation of "*hajime*", stand and start fighting

1. Return to the start line and take *chudan-no-kamae*
2. After the proclamation "*shobu-ari* (match over)", drop into *sonkyo* and sheathe the *shinai*
3. Release the right hand
4. Stand up and take 3-5 steps back to the start point in *taito*
5. Perform *ritsurei* from *sageto* to finish

Gripping the *shinai*

Grip the *tsuka* with the left hand from above. The seam of the *tsukagawa* (leather sheath covering the *tsuka*) runs between the thumb and forefinger. Close the little-finger and ring-finger lightly, and very gently grip with the thumb and forefinger.

The position of the right hand on the *tsuka* can be gauged by placing the *tsukagashira* on the inner-elbow.

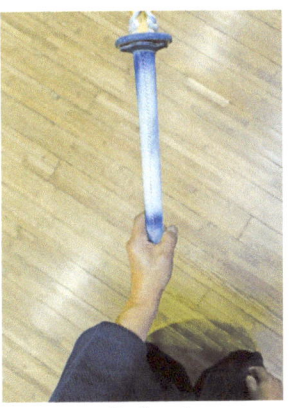 

1. Left grip
2. Position of the right hand

The five *kamae*

There are five basic *kamae*: *chudan*, *jodan*, *gedan*, *hasso*, and *wakigamae*. Generally, only *chudan* and *jodan* are used in modern kendo. *Chudan* is the most suitable stance for defence and attack and it is important to learn this *kamae* first.

Kamae can be divided into *mi-gamae* (physical stance) and *kokoro-gamae* (mental stance), although the term is usually used in reference to *mi-gamae*.

1. *Chudan-no-kamae*

Chudan is the most basic *kamae* and is suitable for defence and attack. Straighten the back and neck and pull your chin in. Take a deep breath and hold it in the lower abdomen. Puff your chest out and relax both shoulders.

Position the left hand about half a fist's width in front of the stomach, and the right hand close to the *tsuba*. Hold the *shinai* with the *tsuru* on top and with the tip of the *shinai* at the height of the opponent's throat. The wrists should not be rigid, and the elbows should lightly touch the torso.

Chudan-no-kamae with *bokuto* (wooden sword) from different angles   *Chudan-no-kamae* with a *shinai*

2. *Jodan-no-kamae*

There are various types of *jodan-no-kamae*, but *morote-hidari-jodan-no-kamae* (two-handed grip with the left foot forward) is standard. From *chudan*, step forward with the left foot with the feeling of trying to overpower the opponent. Raise the right hand to about one fist's width away from the forehead keeping the left hand vertically above the left foot. Observe your opponent from the space between the hands.

3. *Gedan-no-kamae*

From *chudan*, watch the opponent carefully while taking a small step forward with the right foot. Stabilise your body as if sending roots down into the ground, and lower the tip of the *shinai* to the height of the opponent's knees. This mainly defensive stance allows you to respond to changes in the opponent's posture to attack at any time.

4. *Hasso-no-kamae*

Step out with the left foot from *chudan* while keeping the left hand in front of the solar plexus and the right at mouth height. Raise the *shinai* as if going into *jodan* but then rest the hands on the right side instead of above the head. Have the feeling that the sword, body and spirit are "piercing the heavens".

5. *Wakigamae*

From *chudan*, take a big step back with the right foot. Place the left fist on the right hip with the cutting edge of the sword pointing diagonally downwards. The blade should not be visible from the opponent's perspective. As with *gedan*, it is possible to turn the blade to cut from any angle.

Holding a *shinai*

Left side — **Right side** — **Front**

Holding a *bokuto*

Hold the same way as a *katana* with the left hand on the *tsukagashira*, and the right hand about half a fist away.

Left side — **Right side**

Position of the feet

There are two ways to position the feet as shown in Fig. A and Fig. B. In both cases, the toes should be parallel and facing forward. In Fig. A, there is a foot's width between the feet, with the toes of the left foot in line with the heel of the right foot. Fig. B shows a foot's width between the feet, with the right foot about one-and-a-half foot-lengths in front.

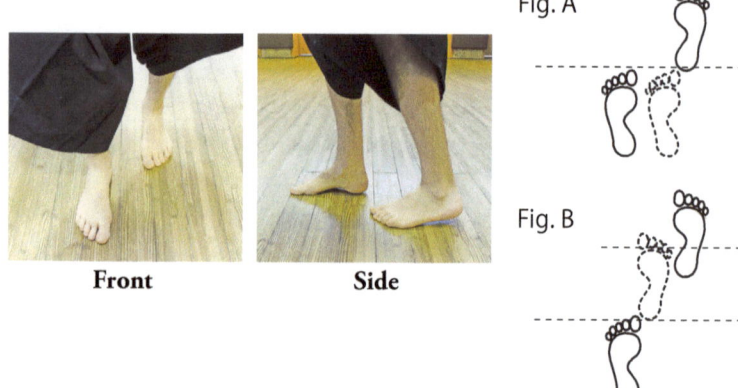

Front **Side**

Fig. A

Fig. B

The eyes

It has always been taught in kendo that the eyes are crucial. For example, the saying, "First eyes, second feet, third spirit, fourth technique" is a well-known adage in kendo. The teaching "*Enzan-no-metsuke*" means to look upon your opponent as if "gazing (*metsuke*) at a far mountain (*enzan*)". That is, to observe all the opponent's movements. Also, "*Kanken futatsu no metsuke*" indicates two ways to look upon one's opponent: "*kan*" and "*ken*". Miyamoto Musashi wrote, "*Kan* is strong and *ken* is weak." Observing the opponent's spirit, their state of mind, is looking inside (*kan*); and observing their *kamae* is looking at the exterior (*ken*).

4. *Ashi-sabaki*—footwork

The feet are used to defend, attack, and execute strikes instantaneously depending on the actions of your opponent. As mentioned above, after the "eyes" come the "feet". To "strike with the feet" rather than relying on upper body strength has been one of the fundaments of swordsmanship since antiquity. *Ashi-sabaki* is also called *tai-sabaki* (body movement). The feet are manoeuvred forward, back, left, right, and diagonally with the following four types of *ashi-sabaki*: *ayumi-ashi*, *okuri-ashi*, *tsugi-ashi* and *hiraki-ashi*.

Ayumi-ashi

Ayumi-ashi is like walking, alternating the left and right feet to move either forward or back. *Ayumi-ashi* can be used to assail your opponent quickly from a distance, upset your opponent's timing by striking with a big swing above the head, or for *hiki-waza* (striking while moving backward).

Okuri-ashi

Okuri-ashi is used to manoeuvre rapidly in any direction with small steps to strike the opponent, or pass through after striking. This is the most widely used form of footwork in kendo.

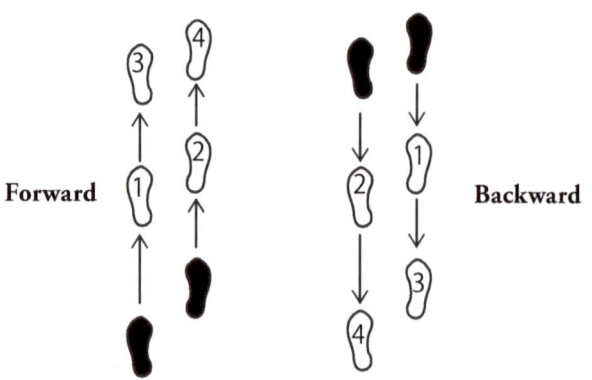

Forward   Backward

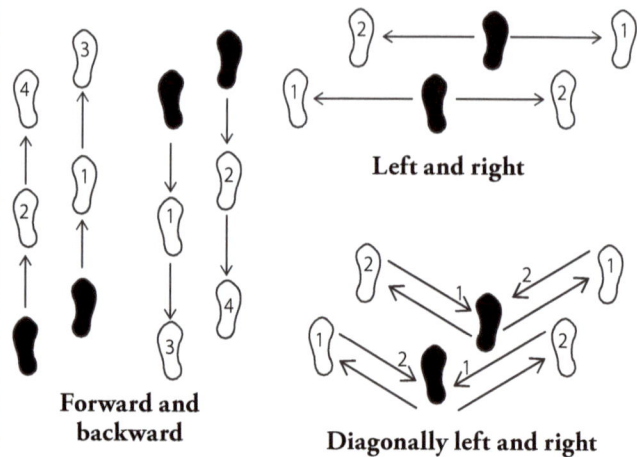

Forward and backward

Left and right

Diagonally left and right

Tsugi-ashi

In *tsugi-ashi* the rear (left) foot is brought forward close to the front (right) foot, enabling a quick advance or strike from the right foot. Alternatively, when retreating, bring the right foot back without moving the left foot. By doing so, the *maai* (the distance between you and the opponent) can be closed without them noticing. *Tsugi-ashi* is therefore also called "*nusumi-ashi*", or "steal-foot". The body or centre of gravity may move up when pulling the left foot in. Your opponent may see this, and will therefore be able to understand your intentions. It is therefore necessary to move in such a way that it does not invite your opponent to strike.

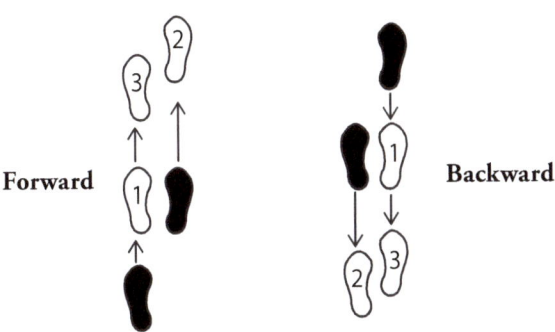

Hiraki-ashi

Hiraki-ashi is footwork that enables the body to be moved diagonally to the left and right to either dodge or defend against an opponent's pressure or strike, or to instigate a counterattack. In *hiraki-ashi,* it is not only the feet that are moved. The body should be moved with the hips in the centre while taking the opponent's centreline.

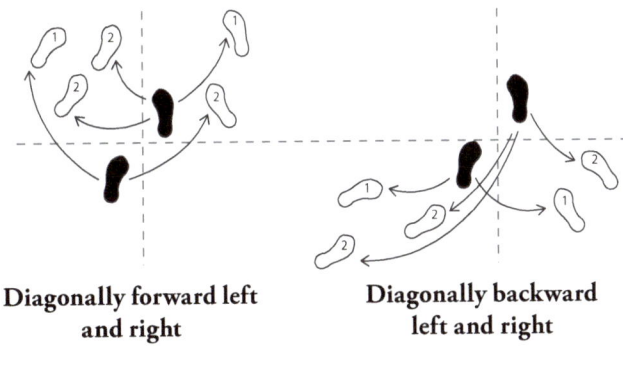

Diagonally forward left and right   **Diagonally backward left and right**

5. *Suburi*—how to swing the *shinai*

Upon learning the general basics and *ashi-sabaki* as described above, it is time to start practising how to strike. The basis of striking is in *suburi*—swinging the *shinai*. The diagram shows that there are eight cutting directions, but in modern kendo, numbers 2, 6, and 8 marked by the dotted line are not used. The cutting directions used today are 1 (top to bottom), 3 (horizontally left), 4 (horizontally right), 5 (top right to bottom left), and 7 (top left to bottom right). First, the correct way in which to swing the *shinai* along the cutting directions must be learnt.

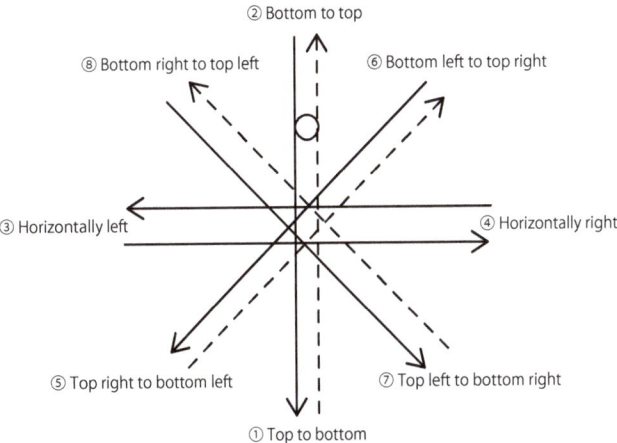

Cutting directions

The *shinai* is held with the right hand in front of the left. Strikes are made with a straight cutting angle with the *monouchi* (the top 10cm of the *shinai*), together with *ki-ken-tai-itchi* (mind, sword and body in unison). Make sure that the shoulders, elbows and wrist joints are sufficiently stretched and warmed up before starting *suburi*.

Straighten the back, take a deep breath and hold it in the lower abdomen, straighten the neck and pull in the chin. Relax the shoulders and arms and place both hands together as if praying, or with the fingers interlocked, as shown in the photographs.

Palms together   **Fingers interlocked**

Take one step forward with the right foot while gently bending the wrists, elbows and shoulders in a big upwards motion. Drop both shoulders, close the armpits, and extend the elbows and wrists as you cut down. The thumbs and forefingers are relaxed while the little, ring, and middle fingers should be tightened. Stop the downward cutting motion in front of the chest while bringing the left foot forward.

Swinging up   **Cutting down (side)**   **Cutting down (side)**   **Cutting down (front)**

Kamae   **Swinging up**   **Cutting down**

Another method is to stagger the hands with the left hand stopping at chest height and the right at shoulder height. Practise *kote* and *doh* strikes in the same way.

Types of *suburi*

Joge-buri—big vertical swings

While stepping back and forth:
a. Make a big swing overhead and then cut down to the knees.
b. Make a big swing overhead and cut to the *men* or *kote* position.
c. Stagger the hands as if holding a *shinai* and make a big swing overhead followed by a cut down to *men* or *kote*.
d. Stagger the hands as if holding a *shinai*, make a big swing overhead followed by a cut down to *men* or *kote*.

Naname-buri—diagonal swings to the left and right

While stepping back and forth:
a. Make a big swing overhead, turn the wrists and cut down to the diagonal left or right.
b. Make a big swing overhead, turn the wrists and cut down to the diagonal left or right onto *men* or *doh*.
c. Make a big swing up and stagger the hands as if holding a *shinai*, turn the wrists and cut down diagonally to the left or right onto *men* or *doh*.
d. Stagger the hands as if holding a *shinai*, make a big swing overhead, turn the wrists and then cut down to *men* or *doh*.

Choyaku-joge-buri, naname-buri – vertical and diagonal swings while jumping

Both a. and b. outlined in the *joge-buri* and *naname-buri* methods can be performed while jumping - *choyaku*. Start with big, slow swings and gradually increase the speed.

Ashi-sabaki and *suburi*

Ashi-sabaki in *suburi* is not only moving backward and forward with *okuri-ashi*. Try *joge-buri* and *naname-buri* with various movements. For example, forward-forward-forward, forward-forward-backward, backward-forward-forward.

Suburi becomes more complex when combined with the various types of *ashi-sabaki* like *tsugi-ashi*, *ayumi-ashi* and *hiraki-ashi*, and stamping the right foot. To maintain stability in the legs, make the shoulder movements big, but keep the elbows and wrist joints as relaxed as possible. Try practising without holding a *shinai*.

How to do *suburi*

Grip the *tsuka* with the right hand positioned in the correct place. The body will naturally lean to the right, which in turn makes the cutting angle diagonally right. This must be avoided. To prevent this, it helps to draw the correct cutting angles on a wall. Then grip the *shinai* with both hands together and trace the five cutting angles with big swings. Gradually move the right hand forward so that it grips the *shinai* in the correct position while being careful to maintain a good posture.

Starting in the same position as 1 in the following photographs, it is also possible to move the body forward or back, and left or right (*hiraki-ashi*). Practise repeatedly so that you can execute *joge* and *naname suburi*.

Joge-buri

Starting in *chudan-no-kamae*, keep the shoulders, elbows and wrists relaxed with the left hand in the centre. Without changing grip, swing the *shinai* overhead in a large, straight motion as if drawing an arc with the tip. With the chest pushed out, drop both shoulders and extend the elbows and wrists to make a big downward cut, keeping both hands on the centreline. With a straight back, grip the *shinai* tightly with the little fingers and stop the downward cut when the left hand is about half a fist away from the navel.

Swinging the *shinai* does not require a lot of power. Make big and relaxed movements to start with and then gradually increase the speed. Also, try swinging the *shinai* up to the *jodan* position, as in photo 3, and cutting down from there.

Front View

1. *Chudan*   **2.** Raise the *shinai*   **3.** Swing high overhead   **4.** Very large back swing   **5.** Cut down   **6.** Stop the cut

Side View

| 2. Raise the *shinai* | 3. Swing overhead | 4. Very large back swing | 5. Cut down | 6. Stop the cut |

Naname-buri

Swing the *shinai* up as in *joge-buri*, but turn the wrists when cutting down. Ensure that both hands do not stray from the centreline, and that the upper body maintains a straight posture. The cutting angle is not excessive.

Naname-buri—cutting down from the right   *Naname-buri*—cutting down from the left

6. How to wear *bogu*—protective armour

It is important that the *kendo-gi*, *hakama*, and *bogu* are all worn properly. Not doing so can be dangerous and prevent you from executing techniques correctly.

How to put on the *keiko-gi*

Tie the cords securely in front of the chest making sure that the lapel is not open. Place both hands inside the *hakama* and pull the *kendo-gi* down at the back so that it does not puff out or wrinkle.

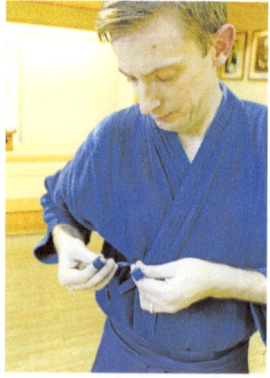  

1. Tightly fasten the cords
2. Tidy the back of the *keiko-gi*
3. Pull the excess portion of the *keiko-gi* down

16

How to put on the *hakama*

The front hem of the *hakama* should be around ankle height. Wrap the front straps around the torso just over the hips. Cross them at the front and then tie at the rear. The small plastic tag attached to the *koshi-ita* (panel at the back of the *hakama*) is tucked inside the straps already around the torso. The *koshi-ita* should be a little higher than the hips. The rear straps are firmly tied at the front in either a bow or reef knot so that the rear of the *hakama* does not drop down.

1. The front straps are wrapped around over the hips and then tied

2. The *koshi-ita* is positioned just above the hips

3. Do not allow the back of the *hakama* to drop

Bow

Reef knot

Folded *keiko-gi*

Folded *hakama*

How to wear *bogu*

Bogu should be put on in the following order: *tare*, *doh*, *men*, then *kote*.

Tare

The *tare* has front and rear panels. The largest of the five panels are in front.
1. Place the *tare* just below the navel, angled diagonally upwards over the upper part of the hips.
2. Cross the straps below the *koshi-ita* and pull tight.
3. Next, wrap the straps around the front and tie under the central front panel of the *tare*.
4. The remaining portion of the straps should be tucked under the *tare*'s smaller panels.

1

2

3

4

Doh

Place the centre of the *doh* on the chest. The bottom edge of the *doh* should be level with the bottom of the *tare* belt.

1. Take the left long cord with the right hand and pass it back over the right shoulder. Thread it through the loop on the right side and fasten. Do the opposite with the cord attached to the right side of the *doh* so that both cords make a cross at the back.
2. The two shorter cords should be slightly slack with the knot tied tightly.

Tenugui (cotton towel)

The *tenugui* is used to keep the hair in place, prevent sweat from running into the eyes, help the *men* stay on the head, and prevent chafing. There are various ways to wear the *tenugui*, but the following method is the most common.

1. Open the *tenugui* and place on top of the head

2. From the back, wrap the upper edge around the front

3. Cross the other side in front

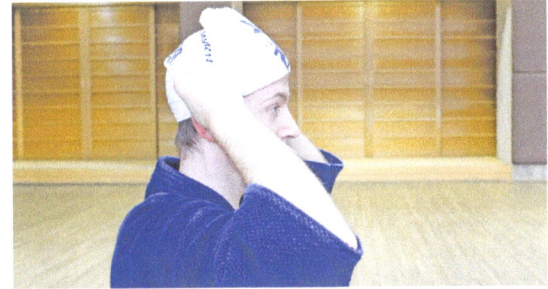

4. Pull the *tenugui* back over the top of the head from the front

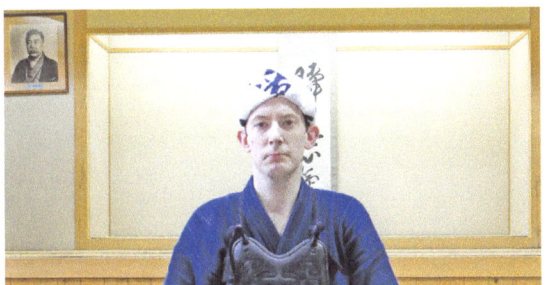
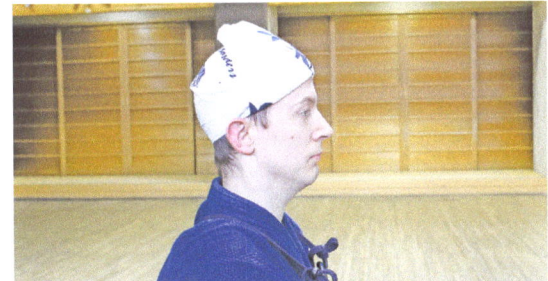

5. Finished

Men

There are two ways to put on the *men*. One way is to attach the cords to the fourth bar from the bottom of the *mengane* (metal grill that protects the face). The other is to attach the cords to the very top of the *mengane*'s vertical bar (known as "*Kansai* style"). The former method will be explained in this book.

First, insert the chin inside the *men*. The *men* should be fixed in a position where the eyes can see through the *monomi* (slightly wider bar space).

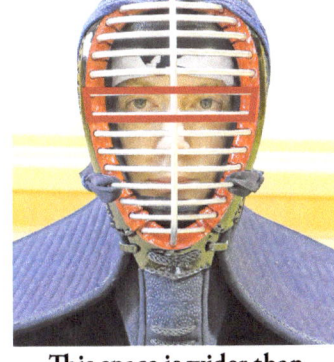

This space is wider than between the other bars. It is called the *monomi* and it enables you to clearly see the opponent.

How to tie the *men*
1. Wrap both the cords around the back of the head under the part of the skull that protrudes, and then pull them tight.
2. Bring both the cords around to the front towards the top of the *mengane*. Next, thread one cord under the vertical bar at the very top of the *mengane* and wrap around the head under the cord that is already there. Repeat with the other cord and tie them tightly in a bow at the back. Adjust them so that the loops and ends are the same length.
3. Open a small space around the ear area of the *men-buton* (padded part of the *men*) so that it is easier to hear. This prevents too much pressure on the eardrums. The *men-dare* (shoulder flaps) should be pulled slightly diagonally forward so that the shoulders are not impeded.

From the top of the vertical bar of the *mengane*

From the fourth-from-bottom bar of the *mengane*

How to put on the *kote*

The left *kote* should be put on first. The palm of the *kote* should fit so that the *shinai* can be gripped with ease. The cords that tie the *kote* together must not be too tight or slack, and the loose ends should be tucked inside.

7. How to store *bogu*

Bogu should be taken off in the following order: *kote*, *men*, *doh* and *tare*.

A set of *bogu* must be treated with care. Damaged *bogu* can result in injury. Do not place the front of the *doh* on the floor as it may get scratched. Dry the *men* and *kote* quickly after practice.

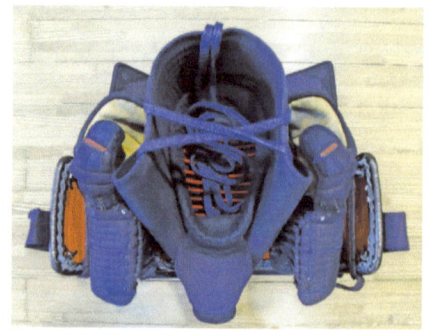

Method of packing *bogu* for storing on a shelf

Method of packing *bogu* for hanging on the wall

SECTION 2
Basic Strikes (*uchi*) and Thrusts (*tsuki*)

The valid striking areas in kendo are illustrated in this diagram.

men: centre-*men*, left-*men*, right-*men*

doh: right-*doh*, left-*doh*

kote: right-*kote*, left-*kote*

tsuki: inko-*tsuki* (throat), *mune-tsuki** (chest)
(*Mune-tsuki is no longer allowed.)

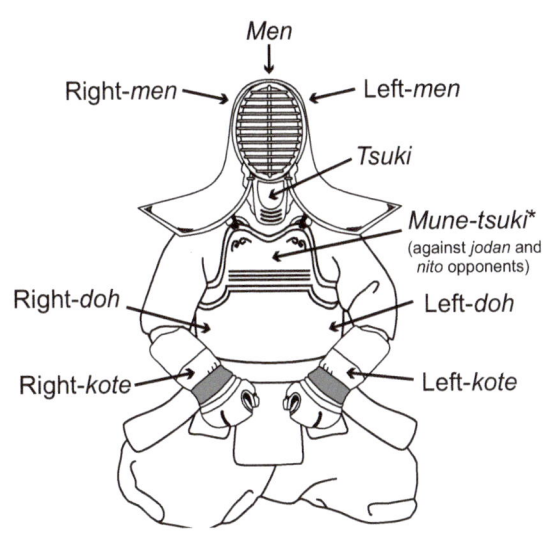

1. How to strike *men*

To strike centre-*men*, apply pressure to the opponent's centreline with the tip of the *shinai* while taking a step forward with the right foot. At the same time, raise the *shinai* in a big motion overhead. When the opponent's *kamae* opens to the right, swing the *shinai* straight down while bringing the left foot forward. Strike with *tenouchi*, that is tightening the grip on the *shinai* at the moment of impact and then loosening immediately afterwards (see below). When striking left- and right-*men*, raise the *shinai* overhead in the same manner as striking centre-*men*, but rotate both wrists either left or right as the strike is made.

1. At *issoku-itto-no-maai* (one-step-one-strike interval) be alert and seek an opportunity to strike

2. Apply pressure to the opponent's centreline while stepping forward with the right foot

3. Make a large swing overhead

4. Cut straight down

5. Bring the left foot forward, and strike with *tenouchi*

Left-*men*		Right-*men*		Centre-*men*

1. Turn both wrists to the right and cut down	2. Drop both shoulders and straighten the back when striking	1. Turn both wrists to the left	2. Strike with both hands stopping in the centre	1. Strike straight as if trying to break through the opponent's centre

Important Points

— Advance by pushing off with the left hip and sliding the right foot along the floor.
— When swinging the *shinai* overhead, move your centre of gravity forward slightly and diagonally upward with the hips.
— When cutting down, do not allow your hands to deviate from the centreline. Strike with the feeling of breaking the opponent's centreline with a vertical cut.
— Raise and lower the *shinai* in one large, straight movement.
— Strike with the little fingers tightened, back straight, shoulders relaxed, elbows and wrists extended.
— Snap the left foot up immediately.

2. How to strike *kote*

To strike right-*kote*, apply pressure to the opponent's centreline with the tip of your *shinai*, take one step forward with the right foot, swing the *shinai* overhead, and without a moment's hesitation bring the *shinai* down to strike as the left foot is snapped up.

1. *Chudan-no-kamae*

2. Apply pressure to the opponent's centre and start to raise the *shinai*

3. Make a large upward swing

4. Snap the left foot up as you strike

Important Points

— While pressuring the opponent's centreline, move in from the left hip and change position from their left side to the right.
— Strike using the whole body, not just the hands.
— With the left fist, strike from above the tip of the opponent's *shinai* with the feeling of trying to split it.
— Make sure that the upper body does not lean to the right side.
— Do not leave the left foot trailing: quickly pull it in.

About *tenouchi*

Both hands and wrists should be flexible and relaxed when gripping the *shinai*. The thumbs should be kept behind the forefingers and the middle finger should grip the *shinai* lightly. The base of the thumbs should push down while the forefingers raise the *shinai* up. In swinging down to strike, the area between the thumbs and forefingers should push as the little fingers strongly pull on the *shinai*.

The right hand grip

   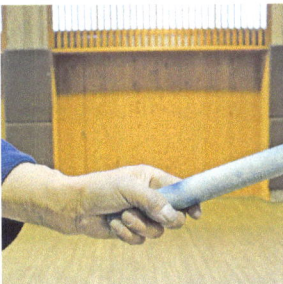

The left hand grip

The *shinai* is manipulated like a lever: the right hand pushes and the left hand pulls. Whether using one hand or two in the strike, it is important to be able to manipulate the *shinai* freely. It is essential to learn correct *tenouchi* for this reason. Try hitting a drum with a short stick, for example, to get the right feeling.

3. How to strike *doh*

To strike right-*doh*, apply pressure to the opponent's centreline with the tip of the *shinai* and step forward with the right foot. Swing the *shinai* up, and when the opponent raises their hands, quickly cut down while pulling the left foot in.

1. Full of energy, look for an opportunity to strike

2. Apply pressure with the tip of the *shinai*

3. Make a large swing overhead

Important Points

— Right-*doh* is faster than *kote*, *men*, and *tsuki* because the striking area is lower. However, it is easier to break one's posture, so take a big step with the right foot to keep the body upright.
— The upper body may lean forward, so put your hips into the strike.
— When swinging overhead then cutting down, make sure that both hands do not deviate from the centre.
— Do not raise the right shoulder up. The tip of the *shinai* is not moved in an excessively big circular motion.
— Refrain from using too much power in the right hand; apply pressure with the left fist as you make a big upward swing of the *shinai*.
— Lift your *shinai* overhead with the left fist as if to raise the tip of the opponent's.

4. Pull in the left foot when striking

4. How to *tsuki*

With the right fist advancing in the direction of the opponent's *tsuki-dare* (*tsuki* target), take one step with the right foot while extending the arms to execute the thrust. The left side of the opponent's *shinai* is called "*omote*" (obverse), and a *tsuki* from this side is known as *omote-tsuki*. Conversely, opponent's right side is called "*ura*" (reverse). A *tsuki* technique executed from this side is *ura-tsuki*. There are two methods for executing a *tsuki* technique: *katate-tsuki* (one-handed) and *morote-tsuki* (two-handed).

1. From *chudan*

Katate-tsuki (*omote*)

Morote-tsuki (*omote*)

2. When the opportunity arises, advance towards the opponent's *tsuki-dare*

3. Quickly thrust out

4. Pull in the left foot

Important Points

— With *morote-tsuki*, the *shinai* is held with the right hand in front. This makes it easy for the left side of the body to lag behind. To learn how stabilise the body it is useful to start with *katate-tsuki*.
— *Katate-tsuki*: Once the opportunity to attack has been created by using the right hand and the tip of the *shinai*, extend the left arm out. The right arm should be pulled back to the right hip.
— *Katate-tsuki*: As the left hand applies *tenouchi* on impact, the right should let go of the *shinai*.
— *Katate-tsuki*: Do not move the right arm outside the body line.
— The arm, left fist, and *shinai* all move in a straight line.
— Bend the right knee and straighten the left leg when doing *katate-tsuki*, but be sure to straighten up as you pull back after contact.
— It is important to thrust with the whole body, not just the hand. Relax both shoulders, and generate power from the waist.
— *Morote-tsuki*: Do not insert too much power in the right fist or shoulder. Straighten the back and relax the shoulders. Turn both hands inwards when thrusting, as if wringing out a wet hand towel.

SECTION 3
Basic Defence

Kaeshi-waza or *oji-waza* techniques are counterattacks. Your training partner learns correct technique execution through being countered as well.

1. Defending against a *men* strike

Against a centre-*men* strike from the *omote* side, move both hands one fist's width outside of the body's centreline to make a triangle with the tip of the *shinai*, the left fist, and the side of the body. Defend by making a triangle in the opposite way against a strike from the *ura* side. Additionally, you can leave the *shinai* in the same position but stand it up so that the opponent's *men* strike can be parried downwards.

Defensive triangles against a centre-*men* attack.

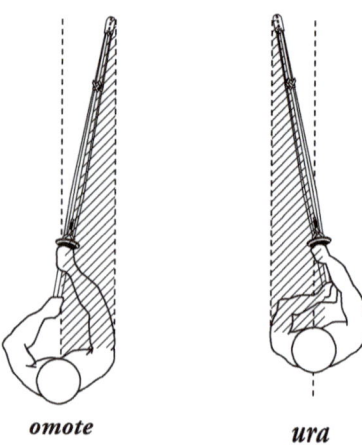

omote   *ura*

From *omote*   **From *ura***

Important Points

— Depending on the *maai* or the speed of the opponent's *shinai*, you can defend by: 1. taking one step forward; 2. staying in the same position; 3. taking one step back; 4. moving the body out of the way.
— Position your body into a triangle with the tip of the *shinai*, the left fist, and the side of the body. Raise the tip of the *shinai* roughly to the height of the opponent's left-*men* when defending on the *omote* side. When defending on the *ura* side, raise the *shinai* to the level of the opponent's right-*men*.
— Assume a suitable posture that allows a counterattack immediately after defending.
— It may be necessary to move back when defending, but constantly go forward mentally.
— Defend with relaxed shoulders and arms.
— By standing the *shinai* up, you can learn parrying techniques against centre, left or right *men* strikes from both the *omote* and *ura* triangle positions discussed above.
— Move the body either left or right and receive the *men* strike with the *shinai* held horizontally, and counterattack by turning the wrists.

2. Defending against a right-*kote* strike

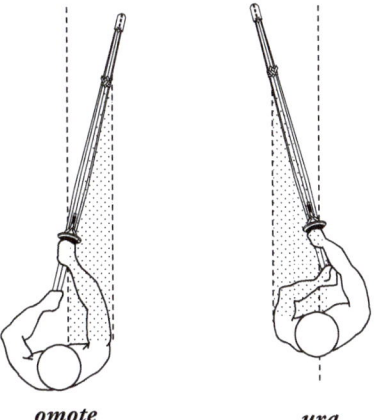

Defensive triangles against a *kote* attack.

omote   ura

1. Against an attack to right-*kote*, turn the right-hand grip slightly to the left, and move the left hand about a fist's width to the left of your centreline or in front of the right hip.
2. Against an attack that comes from above, drop the tip of the *shinai*, move the left hand about a fist's width to the left of your centreline, and defend by allowing the opponent's *shinai* strike your *shinai*.
3. Against an attack that comes from below, drop the tip of your *shinai* diagonally to the right and defend by pushing down onto the opponent's *shinai*.

1. Defend with the triangle made from the *nakayui* and the inside of the left fist

2. Defend against an attack coming from above by parrying

3. Defend against an attack coming from below by pushing down on the *shinai*

3. Defending against a right-*doh* strike

1. Move the left foot forward diagonally left, turn the right hand grip on the *shinai* to the left and shift to the right, move the left fist toward the right hip, and block the strike near the *tsuba*.
2. Move the left foot forward diagonally left, and lift the left fist so that it is diagonally above and in front of the forehead. Bend the left elbow to the right, and use the right hand to support the *shinai* to defend the opponent's strike to right-*doh*.
3. Move the left foot forward diagonally left, and defend by pushing diagonally down to the right with the tip of the *shinai*.

1. Move the *shinai* to the right and use the area near the *tsuba* to defend

2. Defend by parrying

3. Push down on a strike coming from below

4. Defending against *tsuki*

To defend against *tsuki* coming from the *omote* side, turn both hands slightly to the right and raise the *shinai* forward to the diagonal right, deflecting the opponent's *tsuki* with the left side of the *shinai*. For a *tsuki* coming from the *ura* side, turn both hands slightly to the left and raise the *shinai* forward to the diagonal left, deflecting the opponent's *tsuki* with the right side of the *shinai*.

From *omote*

From *ura*

SECTION 4
Kirikaeshi (uchikaeshi)

1. How to perform *kirikaeshi (uchikaeshi)*

Kirikaeshi involves striking centre-*men* followed by left- and right-*men* repeatedly—that is, four left- and right-*men* (starting with the opponent's left) while moving forward, and then five left- and right-*men* while moving backward. After the final left-*men* strike, move back to create space, and then strike centre-*men* to finish. This sequence is usually executed two times.

Kirikaeshi has always been considered the most fundamental exercise in kendo. It trains the kendoka to move efficiently, and increases coordination of the arms and legs. It also builds agility and greater respiratory capacity. Mind, body, and technique become unified. Strikes will become precise and relaxed and balanced. It is a tough exercise but the benefits are great.

It is taught that when doing *kirikaeshi*, "Put all of your spirit into the exercise. Continue wholeheartedly without rest, pushing yourself to the limits of your physical strength and respiration. Strike big and fast, with the hands and feet in unison, and seek an amalgamation of mind and body. Strike furiously, and when the arms are tired and your breathing is exhausted, finish with a centre-*men* strike just as resonant as the first one."

Kirikaeshi is thus a fundamental method for learning how to strike. You will also learn about *maai*, use of the wrists, *tenouchi*, *ashi-sabaki*, breathing, and vocalisation. It is the perfect drill for mastering the basics of kendo, and is therefore crucial that it is practised with big, correct movements.

NEXT PAGE: *Kirikaeshi* – centre-*men*, repeated left- and right-*men*, centre-*men*.

Note: After the centre-*men* strike, usually four strikes are made moving forward and five moving back before the final centre-*men* strike. These photos only show two moving forward and three moving back between the first and last centre-*men* strikes.

Ki-ken-tai-itchi **(mind, sword and body in unison)**

Ki is the action of the mind or spirit, *ken* is the manipulation of the sword and *tai* is the movement of the body. For a strike to be judged valid (*yuko-datotsu*), *ki* (manifestation of one's intent or spirit), *ken* (technique), and *tai* (posture) must be unified at the instant of contact. If a strike is lacking one of these three elements, it will not be valid.

Big and strong, fast and light

Beginners must learn to do kendo with big, strong strikes. They must strive to practise in the correct manner. Doing kendo this way is tiring, but is necessary to develop perseverance and control. Gradually, you will stop using unnecessary power in your techniques, making them focused, fast, and effective.

Shinai manipulation in *kirikaeshi*

1. Above the head, turn to the right **2. Above the head, turn to the left** **3. Strike**

Important Points

— Using the whole body, make the movements as big, fast, and precise as possible.
— Strikes are made with *ki-ken-tai-itchi* with the feeling that each one is valid.
— Beginners can perform *kirikaeshi* with one breath for each strike, but they must always maintain the connection with the opponent and do as a series of movements.
— The left fist is always on the centreline when swinging the *shinai* overhead. Raise the hands high enough so that the top of the opponent's head can be seen from underneath. Keep the shoulders relaxed, and the wrists and *tenouchi* supple. Strikes to left- and right-*men* should be made at an angle of 45°.
— Do not let the left fist stray from the centreline when cutting down. Extend both arms naturally with the left fist in the centre in front of the chest.
— After the first centre-*men* strike, quickly take a deep breath and exhale continuously from the first of the repeated left- and right-*men* strikes through to the final centre-*men* strike.
— Generate energy by screaming loudly, and make the last centre-*men* strike especially vigorous.
— Do not let your spirit and posture wane.

2. How to receive *kirikaeshi*

After receiving the first centre-*men* strike, greet the opponent's *taiatari* (body check) with sufficient force. Then, with *ayumi-ashi*, step back from the left foot and then the right. Place the left fist around hip height, and the right around chest height. Allow the attacker to strike the *shinai*, which is stood vertically and pulled in slightly towards the body.

1. Receiving a left-*men* strike **2. Receiving a right-*men* strike**

Important Points

— Receive the first *men* strike from the *issoku-itto-no-maai* interval.
— When receiving *taiatari*, concentrate power in the lower abdomen and step forward slightly with the right foot. Open by tilting the *shinai* to the right with the left fist in front of the left hip.
— After *taiatari*, quickly take a big step backward with the left foot and receive the strike to left-*men*. When receiving the strike to right-*men*, step back with the right foot with *ayumi-ashi*.
— From *chudan*, stand the *shinai* up and meet the opponent's strike with a firm but relaxed grip. Encourage the attacker to make the left- and right-*men* strikes with *ki-ken-tai-itchi*.

Receiving *men* from *taiatari*

3. Applied practice

1. Assume the correct posture and gauge the *maai*.
   — To strike left- and right-*men* in the same way, start by positioning the right hand close to the left. In this way, practise *uchikaeshi* repeatedly with the receiver standing in the same spot. Aim to strike with correct posture rather than strength.

2. Horizontal *kirikaeshi* – grip the *tsuka* as if holding a *katana*.
   — Straight back, relaxed shoulders, extend both arms while striking horizontally. Both hands must remain on the centreline, with the arms fully extended. Care should be taken with the cutting angle (*hasuji*).
   — Left- and right-*doh* can be struck in the same way. When striking left-*doh*, the receiver should take one big step back with the left foot and turn side-on. Do in reverse when striking right-*doh*. The attacker's hands should keep to the centreline, and the tip of the *shinai* must strike as though cutting through to the centre.
   — Abdominal strength is needed to do horizontal *kirikaeshi*. The back must also be straight, and the shoulders, elbows, wrists and other joints fully employed in the strikes.

1. Left-*men* **2. Right-*men*** **3. Left-*doh*** **4. Raise the *shinai* up** **5. Right-*doh***

3. *Kirikaeshi* is usually done with four steps forward and five steps back. However, the number of strikes and steps can be decided by the receiver. Do each strike as big, fast, and correct as possible for as long as you have breath.

4. *Kirikaeshi* can be executed with left-left-right, right-right-left strikes, or any other pattern.

5. The receiver takes the lead, and can adapt the exercise by moving backward and forward, and to the left and right, diagonally or in any other direction as they see fit.

6. Strikes can be made while moving the body to the left or right sides.

7. Alternate between left and right *men* and *doh*.

8. Use the whole length of the dojo, moving forward and backward for as long as you have breath. This will make your body movements smooth and agile.

9. The receiver can practise striking left- and right-*doh* while being struck on the left- and right-*men*. Change roles and repeat.

10. *Sonkyo-choyaku kirikaeshi*. The receiver moves back and forth striking left- and right-*men*. Squatting down in *sonkyo*, the receiver jumps up to block the strike and then counters with *doh*. This should be repeated continuously to the left and right sides.

11. With *shinai* tips crossing at *issoku-itto-no-maai*, both execute *kirikaeshi* either: 1. standing in the same place; 2. moving backward and forward; 3. both moving to the left and right.

Kirikaeshi is a comprehensive exercise that enables one to learn correct striking, body movement, breathing, and other basics. Practise and devise your own methods for training. This is all for forging strength and spirit.

Kiai

Kiai, manifested through a loud cry or scream, is a mental and physical state in which the mind and body are alert and full of energy. *Kiai* applies pressure on the opponent, and creates equilibrium in mind, body and technique. For beginners, letting out a big *kiai* yell will boost morale and momentum, and can also help create an opening in the opponent's defences. *Kiai* is not merely letting out a loud scream: it consolidates the attack.

Striking opportunities

1. Strike the moment the opponent moves (*degashira*).
2. The moment after you defend the opponent's strike and they have stopped moving.
3. When the opponent is both mentally and physically exhausted, or their strikes are off-target and they cannot regain their composure.
4. Pre-empt the opponent's next *waza* and attack. Avoid their strong point and look for holes in their movement.
5. Attack the opponent as they contemplate their next move.
6. Strike when the opponent's mind and body have come to a standstill.
7. Fluster the opponent and then strike.

Chapter 3
Applied Techniques

After learning the basic techniques, the next step is to master "applied techniques". These are divided into two groups: *shikake-waza* (off-the-mark techniques) and *oji-waza* (counter techniques).

SECTION 1
Shikake-waza

1. Creating an opening with the *shinai* tip

It is possible to strike using a basic technique if an opening suddenly manifests in the opponent's *kamae*. If the opponent's *kamae* is strong and no openings are visible, you need to create striking chances.

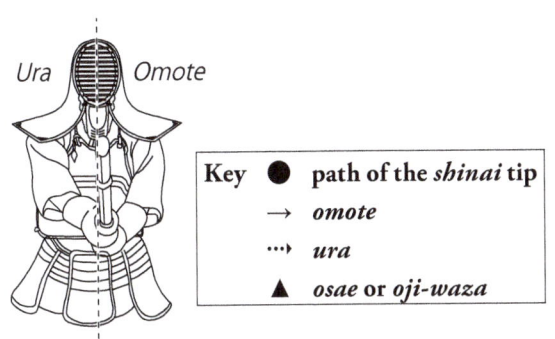

Key
- ● path of the *shinai* tip
- → *omote*
- ⇢ *ura*
- ▲ *osae* or *oji-waza*

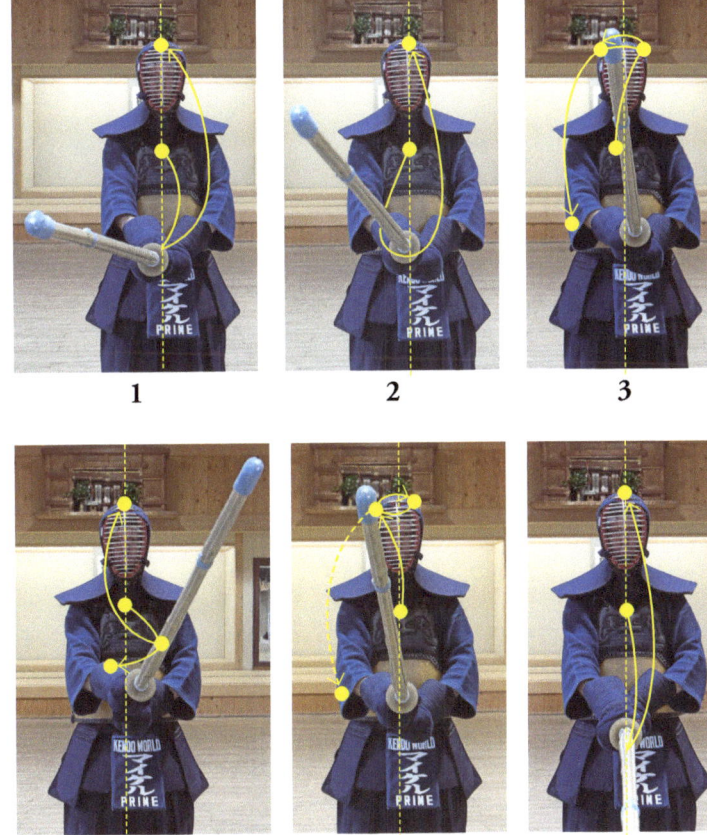

1. Advance as if you are going to attack *kote* from underneath. When the opponent tries to defend, change to the *omote* side.
2. Pressure *kote* from above on the *ura* side. Attack *men* when the opponent tries to defend.
3. Pressure the opponent's left-*men*, and change to the *ura* side when they try to defend.
4. Pressure the opponent's *omote* side, and change to the *ura* side when they try to defend.
5. Pressure the opponent's *ura* side, and change to the *omote* side when they try to defend.
6. Apply pressure by moving the *shinai* down. Strike *men* when the opponent tries to defend.

A. Pressure the opponent's centreline.

To pressure the opponent's centreline, confidently move the tip of the *shinai* towards their *tsuki-dare* or chest as if about to execute *tsuki* while stepping forward with both feet, or just the front foot. Strike the open area when the opponent's *kamae* breaks.

Alternatively, from *chudan*, confidently pressurise the opponent's centreline by moving the *shinai* over the top of the *tsuru* as far as the *naka-yui*. Strike the moment their *kamae* breaks. Move in with the whole body, not just the hands.

1. Strike either centre-, left- or right-*men*, or *tsuki* when the opponent's *kamae* opens.

Pressure the opponent's centre and strike centre-*men*

Pressuring the centreline and attacking with *katate-tsuki* (one-handed *tsuki*)

Pressuring the centreline and attacking with *morote-tsuki* (two-handed *tsuki*)

2. Strike right-*doh* as the opponent raises their hands.

When striking right-*doh*: 1. Move the right foot forward as you strike, and pass the opponent by on the left; 2. Move the left foot forward as you strike and quickly bring the right foot forward as you pass on the left side; 3. Move the right foot forward slightly as you shift your body to the right and strike, and then pass by the opponent on the right. Practise these three ways of striking *doh*. In the case of 1 and 2, *motodachi* should first take a step back with the right foot. This will allow the opponent to advance and have room to execute the technique correctly. Facing straight ahead, *motodachi* takes a step back after receiving the strike and allows the opponent to pass.

Pressure the opponent's centre and strike *doh*:

1. Advance from the right foot, strike, and pass on the (your) left.

2. Move the left foot forward, strike, and pass on the (your) left

3. Move the right foot to the right, strike, and pass on the (your) right

3. Strike right-*kote* when the opponent's hands lift up.

Important Points

— To strike right-*kote*, shift the *shinai* slightly to the left without raising it too much. Advance the right foot to the diagonal left of the centreline and strike.
— Keep the right fist on the centreline, and do not raise the *shinai* tip. The grip on the *shinai* is relaxed. Attack as if executing a *tsuki* technique. This means starting with the *shinai* moving forward, not up.
— Pressuring the centreline, attack from the shortest distance as the opponent raises their hands. Keep your *shinai* parallel to the opponent's and drop it slightly as you move in for the attack from the *omote* side to the *ura* side.
— Do not think about striking strongly with the hands. Strike with the right foot.
— After striking, pass by the opponent and turn quickly. Point the tip of the *shinai* at the opponent's *tsuki-dare* and be ready for the next attack (*zanshin*).
— After being struck, the *motodachi* should stand their *shinai* up and take a big step back with the left foot. This will enable the opponent to execute the technique and demonstrate *zanshin* easily.

4. Strike the moment the opponent uses their *shinai* to defend by pushing down (*osae*).

Change from *omote* to the *ura* side, and strike centre- or right-*men*, or execute *ura-tsuki*.
After striking, move past the opponent and demonstrate *zanshin*. In the case of *tsuki*, take a big step back, assume *chudan* and show *zanshin*.

Tsuki from *omote* to *ura*

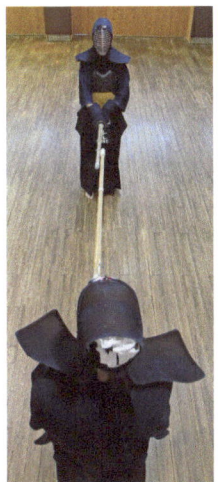     

Centre-*men* from *omote* to *ura*

Important Points

— When changing from *omote* to *ura* for the *men* strike, shift the left fist diagonally forward and move over the opponent's *shinai*.
— When attempting *ura-tsuki*, change from *omote* to *ura* from below. Thrust from the hips.
— After striking *men*, move forward swiftly to the area behind the opponent. Upon reaching a suitable distance past the opponent, turn 180° from the left hip and demonstrate *zanshin*.
— After executing *tsuki*, absorb the forward momentum with the right knee and then push back. Take a big step back with the left foot to create distance. Return the left fist back to the front of the abdomen and assume *chudan*. Always demonstrate *zanshin*.

5. If the opponent presses down on your *shinai* to defend, change to the *ura* side from above and strike right-*men* or right-*kote*.

Strike right-*men*

Strike right-*kote*

Important Point

— To change from *omote* to *ura* when the opponent pushes down on the *shinai*: 1. Move the right fist up diagonally forward with the *shinai* positioned alongside the opponent's; 2. With the right fist on the centreline, change direction as in *oji-kaeshi*.

> ### Ken-tai-itchi
>
> In this case, "*ken*" refers to offence and "*tai*" defence. The meaning of the phrase is that offence and defence should be as one. So, defence is for the purpose of offence, and offence must be for defence.
>
> If you have a mind-set only for attack, you will be struck the instant you start to move. Similarly, if you are preoccupied with defence, when an opportunity arises to strike you will be unable to react and will be struck yourself. This can also be expressed as "*ken-chu-tai*" (defence in offence) and "*tai-chu-ken*" (offence in defence).

B. Pressure the opponent's left chest area.

Pressurise the opponent's left chest from the *omote* side by extending the tip of the *shinai* and stepping in. When their *kamae* breaks to the left, strike centre- or right-*men*, right-*kote* from the *ura* side, or do *ura-tsuki*.

Pressure the opponent's left chest area

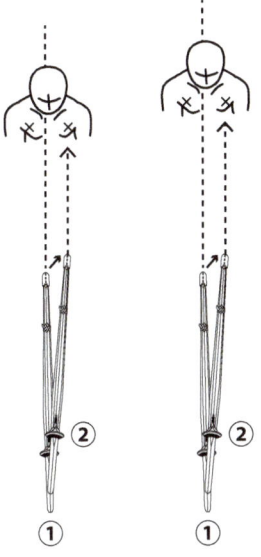

Strike *kote*   ***Ura-tsuki***

Important Points
— Do not apply pressure to the opponent's left chest with the hands only. Put your whole body and feeling into it.
— Slide the *shinai* along the opponent's and move it above or below with the shortest movement to strike right-*kote*.

C. Pressure the opponent's diagonal left-*men*.

To unsettle the opponent's *kamae*, advance as if to strike the opponent's diagonal left-*men*, or move diagonally to the right and from below to make the opponent raise their hands. Then strike centre- or right-*men*, *kote*, or right- or left-*doh*.

Pressure the opponent's left-*men* and strike *kote*

Important Points
— When striking the opponent's diagonal left-*men*, stop just before making contact or let them receive the strike. Change direction immediately after and strike right-*men* or right-*doh*.
— When striking right-*kote*, return the *shinai* to your centreline in one breath.

D. Pressuring the opponent's *kote* from above.

Apply pressure to the opponent's right-*kote* from above. The moment they try to defend: 1. Change to the *omote* side from above; 2. Or, in a circular motion, take the centreline on the *omote* side from below and strike centre- or left-*men*.

Strike centre-*men*

Important Point

— Pressure the opponent's right-*kote* from above stopping just before to break their *kamae*.

E. Pressure the opponent's right-*kote* or abdomen from below.

Lower the *shinai* tip and pressurise the opponent from below by turning it towards their right-*kote*, left fist, or the lower right abdomen. When their *kamae* breaks to their right side, strike centre- or left-*men*, or execute an *omote-tsuki*.

Omote-tsuki

Strike centre-*men*

2. Creating openings through body movement

It is difficult to take a point if both competitors maintain perfectly straight *kamae*. The following is an explanation of how to use the body to cut across the opponent's centreline, or conversely, how to take the opponent's centreline to create a striking opportunity.

A. Move forward to the diagonal right.

When your opponent follows, immediately return to the original position and take the centre. With the opponent's centreline now controlled, strike centre-*men*, right-*kote*, or *tsuki* from the *ura* side.

Striking right-*kote*

Footwork for moving forward diagonally right

Striking centre-*men*

Ura-tsuki

Important Points

— Without breaking *chudan*, stabilise the legs and move the body from the hips.
— Move forward to the diagonal right, and direct the *shinai* tip with the feeling of executing a *tsuki* technique.
— Moving forward to the diagonal right can be done quickly or slowly, but the return should be done quickly in one breath and as one movement.
— When moving forward to the diagonal right, the right foot moves but the left remains where it is. The right foot is then quickly returned to its original position over the centreline.

B. Move forward to the diagonal left.

When the opponent follows, immediately return to the original position over the centreline. With the opponent's centre taken, strike centre-*men* or *omote-tsuki*.

Striking centre-*men*

Important Points

— When moving forward to the diagonal left, it is important to keep the hips on the centreline and add pressure as if about to execute an *omote-tsuki* or a strike to right-*kote*.
— Move the body forward to the diagonal left slowly, but quickly when moving back to the original position.

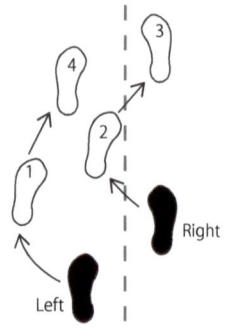

Footwork for moving forward diagonally left

C. Pressure the opponent's centre and move forward to the diagonal right.

With the opponent's centre taken, strike centre-*men*, right- or left-*doh*, or *omote-tsuki*.

1. Pressure the opponent's centre

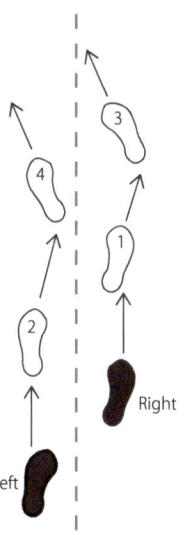

Footwork for pressuring the opponent's centre

2. Do *omote-tsuki*   **2. Strike right-*doh***   **3. Strike centre-*men***

Important Points

— Pressure the opponent's centre in a small, sharp movement, and then quickly move forward to the diagonal right to take the centreline.
— To prevent the upper body becoming twisted and leaning to the left, be sure to relax the arms, and move from the hips.
— The following three ways of movement should be learnt when striking left-*doh*:
  1. Step out with the right foot and move forward to the diagonal right.
  2. Step out with the right foot and move forward to the diagonal left.
  3. Step out with the left foot and move forward to the diagonal left.
     Furthermore, when moving forward to the diagonal right, your opponent will often try to strike your *men* immediately. Bear this in mind, and practise dealing with this occurrence.

1. Step out with the right foot and move forward to the diagonal right

2. Step out with the right foot and move forward to the diagonal left

3. Step out with the left foot and move forward to the diagonal left

D. Apply pressure to the opponent's centre and move forward to the diagonal left.

Controlling the centreline, strike *men*, right-*kote*, left- or right-*doh*, or *ura-tsuki*.

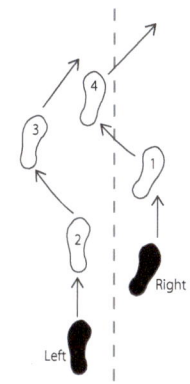

Footwork for pressuring the opponent's centre

Step out with the right foot and move forward to the diagonal right

Attacking right-*kote*

Attacking right-*doh*

Attacking right-*doh* with the left foot in front and the right following

E. To create an opening, move the body left or right, forward or backward, three times in succession to break the opponent's *kamae* or take their centreline.

1. Forward to the diagonal right (slow)—forward to the diagonal left (quick)—return to original position (quick).
2. Forward to the diagonal right (slow)—back to the diagonal left (quick)—forward to the diagonal right (quick).
3. Back to the diagonal left (slow)—forward to the diagonal right (quick)—return to original position (quick).
   Use movements like these to break the opponent's *kamae* or take their centreline, and then strike centre-, left- or right-*men*, left- or right-*doh*, right-*kote* or *tsuki*.

Attacking right-*kote*

Striking *men* continuously or attacking right-*doh*

Important Points

— Make the first movement slow and the second and third quick to break the opponent's *kamae*, take the centreline, and strike.
— Do not use only the hands. Use the hips as you apply pressure, and employ footwork with confidence to exert control over the opponent.
— Do not stop after just one strike. For example, strike right-*kote* and then *men*, *tsuki* and then *men*, or *men* and then *doh*. Practise using other techniques as well.

F. Move forward and backward to take the opponent's centreline and create an opening.

1. Move forward (take the opponent's centre) – move back (move the *shinai* tip out from the centre and point it towards the opponent's left chest area) – move forward (take the opponent's centre from above) – from the *omote* side strike centre-*men* or change to the *ura* side and strike right-*men*.
2. Move forward (take the opponent's centre) – move back (the left foot should move slightly to the left when moving back, drop the *shinai* tip, and change from the opponent's *omote* to *ura* side) – move forward (take the opponent's centre) – from the *ura* side strike centre-*men* or right-*kote*.

F2: Strike centre-*men* from the *ura* side

Important Points

— In the case of F1, when moving forward and backward it is important to pay attention to the *maai* while seizing your optimal *uchima* (striking distance) and dominating the centre.
— In the case of F2, to take the opponent's centre and create an opening use the tip of the *shinai* and then the feet when moving forward and back, manoeuvring the *shinai* tip up and down slightly as the direction is changed.
— With *choyaku-suburi*, move your centre quickly from the legs, and making use of the recoil in the leg muscles you should be able to strike from further away.

Jiri-itchi (unification of technique and theory)

"*Ji*" refers to techniques or technical methodology, whereas "*ri*" refers to the reason and theory behind sword usage. If you do not know the theory of the sword, kendo is simply a physical exercise moving the hands and feet. You will not understand the theory to win. Even if you do know the theory but are unable to match this with the physical techniques, this is also futile. *Ji* and *ri* should be thought of as two wheels of a car: without *ji* there cannot be *ri*, and without *ri* there cannot be *ji*. Therefore, if technique (*ji*) and theory (*ri*) are unified, you will be able acquire a real victory.

3. Creating a *debana* striking opportunity

A. Move the *shinai* tip out of the way to invite an attack.

Being full of spirit and without wanting to retreat, apply pressure on the opponent incrementally. Quickly move the *shinai* tip away from the centreline towards the left chest area of your opponent, thereby creating an opening for them to strike. When your opponent comes in to attack, strike their *men* or *kote*.

Attacking *men*

Attacking *kote*

Important Points

— Synchronise your movement with your opponent (*aiki*) and then momentarily change the rhythm.
— Apply pressure and creep forward from the toes into *uchima*.
— Do not think about striking with the hands, but with the intent of breaking the opponent's centre with your whole body.
— When shifting the *shinai* tip away from the centreline, take care not to move it outside the opponent's body line.

B. Stepping forward and back to make an opponent attack.

Repeatedly step forward and back; then while stepping back, slightly lower your *shinai* tip to invite an attack. Just as the opponent starts to attack, strike centre-*men* or left- or right-*men*, *kote* or *doh*

Attacking *kote*

Attacking right-*men*

Attacking right-*doh*

Important Points

— When moving forward or back, do not think about blocking the opponent's attack. Always be ready to strike.
— When moving back and dropping the *shinai* tip to invite an attack, practise shifting the left foot diagonally back to the left or right but still pointing to the opponent's centreline, and strike the moment the opponent moves.
— Do not pull the left foot back when moving back. Instead, pull the right foot back (*tsugi-ashi*) to "steal the *maai*" and strike the moment the opponent moves.
— To create an opening, move forward and back with *choyaku-suburi* footwork, kicking off with the left foot.

C. Make your opponent attack by moving diagonally left and right, forward and back.

Move freely forward and back, or to the diagonal left and right, striking at the instant your opponent moves.

Attacking centre-*men* from the *omote* side

Important Points

— Keep the arms relaxed and manoeuvre from the hips. Let the opponent take the centre thereby creating an opening to strike *debana*.

— Refrain from moving with a constant rhythm.

The three types of *sen* (initiative)

Sen-no-sen (sen-sen-no-sen)

This initiative is where you sense that the opponent is about to move, and strike immediately as they start. As this involves striking just before the opponent does, it is known as *sen-no-sen* (taking the initiative before the opponent's initiative).

Sen (tai-no-sen—against sen)*

Sensing that the opponent is going to attack, you attack at the same time and beat them to it. Even though you are striking simultaneously, the initiative was yours which is why you win. It is also known as "*tai-no-sen*" (opposite initiative).

Go-no-sen (tai-no-sen—waiting sen)*

When the opponent sees an opening in your *kamae* and moves to attack first, deflect their strike with, for example, *uchiotoshi*. Or, when you perceive a weakening in their spirit, strike forcefully to take advantage. Because you wait for the opponent to start a technique, *go-no-sen* (after initiative) is also known as "*tai-no-sen*" (waiting initiative).

* "*Sen*" and "*go-no-sen*" are also known as "*tai-no-sen*". Although it is pronounced the same (*tai-no-sen*), the *kanji* used in each instance has a different meaning - "against" and "waiting" respectively.

4. Creating an opening by suppressing the opponent's *shinai* and taking the centreline

A. Suppressing the opponent's *shinai* with *uchiotoshi-waza*.

Uchiotoshi-waza involves striking the opponent's *shinai* down diagonally from above, or to the left or right from either the *omote* or *ura* sides to take the centreline and create an opening.

Note: This technique is generally called *harai-waza* (striking the *shinai*), or as a form of *kaeshi-waza* it is called *uchiotoshi-waza*. Either as a type of *shikake-waza* or *kaeshi-waza*, the movement involves striking the opponent's *shinai* down which is why it is called *uchiotoshi-waza* here.

The following diagrams show the trajectory the *shinai* tip should take in *uchiotoshi-waza*.

| From *ura* | From *omote* | From *omote* or *ura* to *men* or *doh* | From *ura* to *kote* | From *omote* to *kote* |

Uchiotoshi from the *ura* side to a centre-*men* strike

Uchiotoshi from the *omote* side to a centre-*men* strike

Uchiotoshi from the *omote* side to a right-*doh* strike with the right or left foot in front   (left foot in front)

Uchiotoshi from the *omote* side to a right-*men* strike on the *ura* side

Uchiotoshi from the *ura* side to a centre-*men* strike on the *omote* side

Important Points

- Keep the wrists and *tenouchi* flexible, but tighten your hands the instant you hit the opponent's *shinai*. Then relax the grip, and tighten once again at the point of impact when making a strike.
- Advance with the right foot at the same time as hitting the opponent's *shinai*. Then take another step forward with the right foot when making the ensuing strike.
- Do not make the *uchiotoshi* movement too large, and do not move the *shinai* tip outside the opponent's body line. "Kill" the opponent's *shinai* tip and strike immediately.
- Before going on to strike *men*, *doh* or *tsuki*, the *shinai* tip should move from the opponent's left shoulder down to their right hip from the *omote* side. From the *ura* side, the *shinai* tip is shifted from the opponent's right shoulder down to their left hip. If done with a crisp, small movement, the opponent's *shinai* tip will be sufficiently removed from the centre. In other words, you do not need much power.
- Hit the area between the *nakayui* and *tsubamoto* with the *monouchi*.
- If the opponent's *shinai* stays down after being struck, just move in and strike from the *omote* side. If the opponent's right grip is too tense, their *shinai* will immediately return to the original position. In that case,

change from *omote* to *ura*, or *ura* to *omote*, and follow through to strike. For example, strike right-*men* from *ura* when doing *uchiotoshi* from the *omote* side, just as in *kirikaeshi*.

— To strike right-*kote*, the *shinai* tip moves from the opponent's left chest area to below the right fist in a short, sharp, diagonal movement. Strike the moment they return their *shinai* to the *omote* side.
— Practise *uchiotoshi* and *shikake-waza* using the whole body. For example, move forward to the diagonal right. Then execute *uchiotoshi* as you return to the original centreline position, followed by a strike to centre-*men*, right-*men* or *kote*.
— Practise *uchiotoshi* while stepping forward. Or, when the opponent advances, you can take a step back, or to the diagonal left or right rear, and then strike *men*, *doh*, or right-*kote*.

B. Deflecting the opponent's *shinai* with *suriage-waza*.

Suriage-waza are techniques used to deflect the opponent's *shinai* from below by raising the *shinai* diagonally from either the *omote* or *ura* sides.

The following diagrams show the trajectory of the *shinai* tip in *suriage-waza*.

  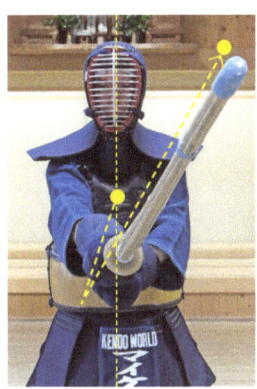 

From *omote* and *ura*   ***Omote***   ***Ura***   ***Suriage* to a *kote* strike**

Suriage from the *ura* side to a centre-*men* strike on the *ura* side

Suriage from the *ura* side to a *kote* strike on the *ura* side

Suriage from the *omote* side to a right-*men* strike on the *ura* side

Suriage from the *omote* side to a right-*doh* strike on the *ura* side

Important Points

— The movement of the *shinai* tip in *suriage-waza* is almost the opposite of *uchiotoshi*. From the *omote* side, the *shinai* tip moves from the left hip diagonally upwards to the right; from the *ura* side, from the right hip diagonally upwards (and forward) to the left.

— In the case of *kote* or *tsuki*, the *shinai* tip should change from the *omote* to *ura* side to the opponent's left chest area to take the centreline.

— Take a deep breath and hold the tension in the lower abdomen. Straighten the neck and pull in the chin. Using the wrists and *tenouchi*, softly snap the grip on the *shinai* and use the *shinogi* to execute *suriage*, and then strike with the whole body.

— If *suriage* is executed from the *omote* side, strike from the *omote* side. If done from the *ura* side, strike on the *ura* side. Practise changing direction.

— When doing *suriage* from the *omote* side, strike on the *ura* side if the opponent changes direction, and vice-versa.

— It is also important to insert the body into the *suriage* movement; or to do *suriage* and then make the strike while moving the body.

— Do not relinquish your guard after one strike—be ready to make another.

C. Suppressing the opponent's *shinai* with *harai-waza*.

Harai-waza is used from below from either the *omote* or *ura* sides to knock the opponent's *shinai* up and off-centre.

The following diagrams show the *shinai* tip trajectory for *harai-waza*.

  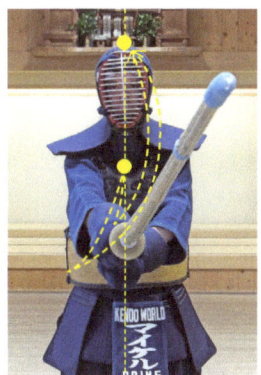 

From *omote* and *ura*   From *omote*   From *ura*   From *ura*

Harai from *omote* to a centre-*men* strike

Harai from *ura* to a right-*kote* strike

Harai from *omote* to a right-*doh* attack (with the left foot forward and passing on the left)

Harai from *omote* to a left-*doh* attack

Important Points

— In creating an opening for *men* and *doh*, the *shinai* tip should move in a large motion: From the *omote* side, move the *shinai* tip to the left side of the opponent's centreline as if drawing a semi-circle. From the *ura* side, drop the *shinai* tip and change to the *omote* side, toward the right side of the opponent's centreline. Move the *shinai* tip as if drawing a semi-circle. In both cases, the action should be made from below to above to force the opponent's *shinai* upwards.

— When executing *harai-waza*, the *shinai* tip should not deviate too far from the opponent's centreline. It should move diagonally upwards from below, and hit the opponent's *shinai* with the side of the *monouchi*.

— In creating an opportunity to strike right-*kote* or *ura-tsuki*, keep the wrists flexible and slide the *shinai* up the opponent's. Change from the *omote* to *ura* side, in a short, sharp semi-circular motion, just in front of the opponent's *tsuba* to take the centre.

D. Suppressing the opponent's *shinai* with *osae-waza*.

In *osae-waza*, the opponent's *shinai* is pressed down from either the *omote* or *ura* sides from above, diagonally downwards, or sideways to take the centreline.

The following diagrams show the trajectory that the *shinai* tip should take to execute *osae-waza*.

Osae to men or *tsuki*　　**From *ura* to men, doh or *tsuki***　　**From *omote* to men**

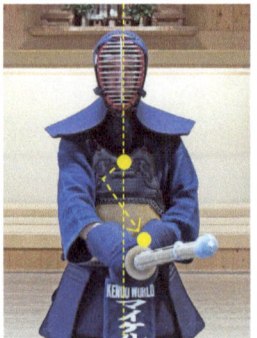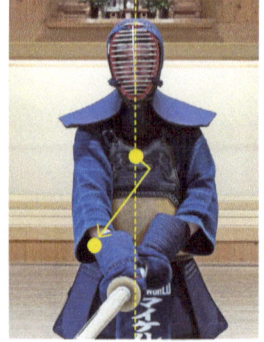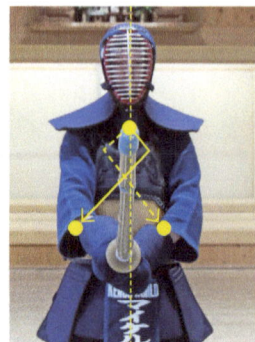

From *ura* to *kote*　　**From *ura* to men or *tsuki***　　**From *ura* to *doh***　　**Osae from *omote* and *ura***

Osae from the *ura* side and strike *men* on the *omote* side as the opponent pushes back

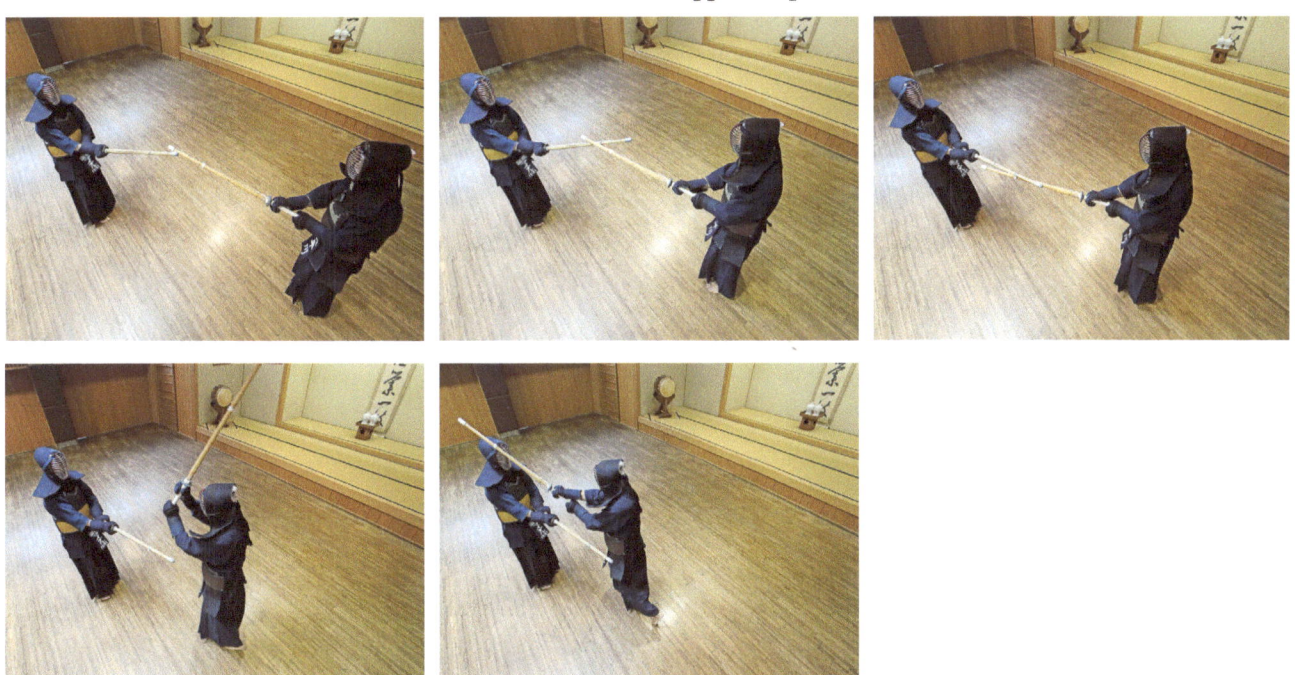

Osae from the *omote* side and strike right-*men* on the *ura* side as the opponent pushes back

Osae from the *omote* side and do *ura-tsuki* as the opponent pushes back

Osae from the *omote* side and strike right-*kote* as the opponent pushes back

Osae from the *omote* side and strike right-*doh* as the opponent pushes back

Important Points

— When attempting to *osae* the opponent's *shinai* from the *omote* side, push the *shinai* tip from their left hip inwards, or from their right hip from the *ura* side. Never move the *shinai* away from the opponent's body.

— The opponent must be made to raise their hands to strike *doh*. Press down on the opponent's *shinai* strongly, diagonally from top to bottom from the *nakayui* to the area below the *tsuba*.

— To create an opening for *kote*, move the opponent's *shinai* (about a *shinai*'s width) diagonally downwards or sideways. Strike *kote* the moment the opponent tries to return their *shinai*.

— After taking the centreline, the opponent will try to defend by returning their *shinai*. Therefore, when doing *osae* from the *omote* side, strike on the opponent's *ura* side, and vice-versa.

— When using *osae-waza* to strike *doh*, if the opponent does not raise their hands sufficiently, apply pressure by honing in on their *men* but stop just before impact and immediately strike *doh*. This is done in one breath.

— Use the whole body, not just the hands, when employing *osae-waza*.

E. Overpower the opponent's *shinai* with *hari-waza*.

Hari-waza (not *harai-waza*) is used to knock the opponent's *shinai* to the side from either *omote* or *ura* to take the centreline. From the *omote* side, the opponent's *shinai* is knocked from right to left and from the *ura* side, left to right.

The following diagrams show the *shinai* trajectory for *hari-waza*.

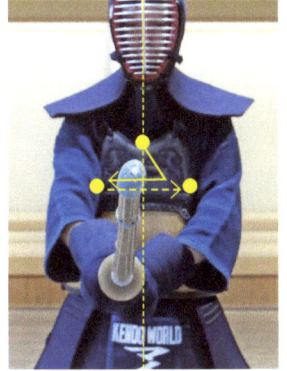 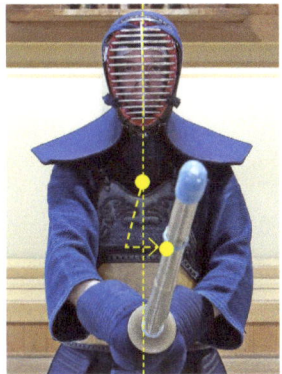 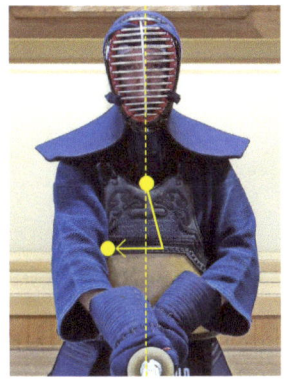 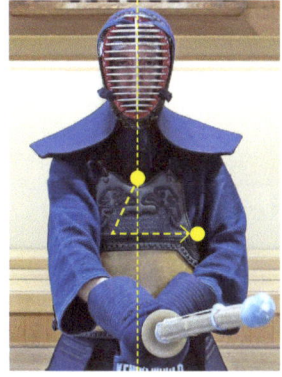

Hari-waza to *men* or *tsuki* from *omote* or *ura* | From *ura* to a *kote* strike | From *omote* to a *men* strike or *tsuki* | *Hari-waza* from *ura* to a *men* or *kote* strike, or *tsuki*

Hari from *omote* to a centre-*men* strike

Hari from *ura* to a centre-*men* strike

Hari from *ura* to a right-*kote* strike

Important Points

— To create an opening for either *men* or *tsuki*, the right fist serves as a fulcrum and should not move from the centreline. To *hari* from the *omote* side, move the left hand one-fist's width to the left side of the centreline and quickly return it knocking the opponent's *shinai* sideways. To *hari* from the *ura* side, drop the *shinai* to change from *omote* to *ura*, and using the right hand as a fulcrum, move the left fist from left to right to knock the opponent's *shinai* to the side.

— Contact on the opponent's *shinai* is made between the *nakayui* and *tsuba*, but not with excessive power, and not just with the hands.

— Keep your grip on the *shinai* relaxed and take a big step forward with the right foot. As the left foot follows, tighten the grip to *hari*. As the centreline is taken, relax the grip slightly and then tighten again when striking *men*.

— To strike *kote*, change from *omote* to *ura* under the opponent's *shinai*. Grip the *shinai* strongly and when the tip points to the opponent's left chest area, take the centre and strike.

— Never move the right hand away from the centreline, or the tip of the *shinai* outside of the opponent's body.

— *Hari-waza* is a horizontal movement, but if the opponent does not raise their hands it is difficult to strike *doh*. Hone in on the opponent's *men* and when they raise their hands, immediately change and strike *doh*.

— Also, practise introducing various body movements into *hari-waza*, and attempt follow-up strikes (*renzoku-waza*).

F. Suppress the opponent's *shinai* with *maki-waza*.

From either the *omote* or *ura* side, bind the *shinai* around the opponent's to take the centreline.

The following diagrams show the *shinai* trajectory for *maki-waza*.

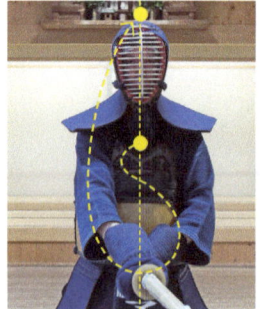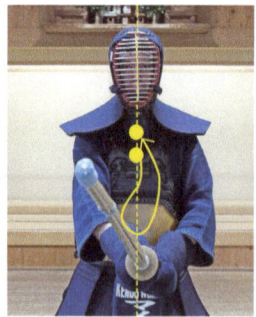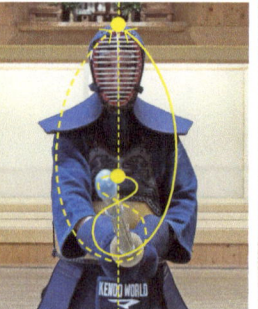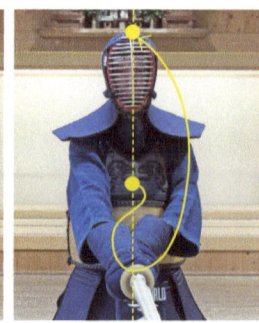

| From the *ura* side to a *men* strike | From the *omote* side to *tsuki* | From the *ura* side to *kote* or *tsuki* | *Maki-waza* to a *men* strike | From the *omote* side to *men* or *tsuki* |

Maki-waza from the *ura* side to a centre-*men* strike

Maki-waza from the *omote* side to a centre-*men* strike

Maki-waza from the *omote* side to a right-*doh* strike

Important Points

— When attempting *maki-waza* from the *omote* side, angle the cutting edge of the *shinai* diagonally down to the left. Then, from the right side of the opponent's centreline, bind the opponent's *shinai* and take the centre as if drawing a circle with the tip. From the *ura* side, move the *shinai* in a circular motion to the left.
— Keep the wrists flexible, the hips centred, and bind the opponent's *shinai* in one breath.
— Do not just bind the tip of the opponent's *shinai*. Move your whole body to bind the *shinai* all the way up to the *tsuba-moto*.
— Try to render the opponent's hands powerless by wrapping their *shinai* twice, entering the *maai*, and striking.
— Do not execute this technique half-heartedly.

5. Creating an opening with *ni / san-dan renzoku-waza* (continuous strikes)

The *shikake-waza* techniques explained above show how to create an opportunity to strike by controlling the opponent's *shinai* or breaking their *kamae* first. Another method to create an opening is by using *ni / san-dan-waza* (two or three stage techniques), of which there are two types:

1. Aim to hit with the first strike, but if it misses a second strike is used to hit the opponent.
2. The first strike is used to pressure the opponent or to invite them to move. As they react, a second strike seizes the resulting opening.

It is essential to keep the attack going until scoring in *renzoku-waza*. The ability to change striking direction between *omote* and *ura*, and the rhythm of small or big techniques, as well as quick footwork, a strong body, and a resolute spirit are necessary to make the technique work.

When attempting *renzoku-waza*, you must commit mentally and physically to the first strike with enough confidence to score. Even though it is called *ni / san-dan-waza* or *renzoku-waza*, it is not necessarily the final blow that will determine victory or defeat: each strike must be made with full spirit and intent.

Nidan and *sandan waza* diagrams
The *nidan* and *sandan waza* will be explained via a series of diagrams. The following is the key:

- **O** (*omote*) The left side of your *shinai* and the right-side of the opponent's when facing them in *chudan*.
- **U** (*ura*) The right-side of your *shinai* and the left-side of the opponent's when facing them in *chudan*.
- ⟶ Step forward and strike the moment the opponent steps back.
- → Small step forward and strike if the opponent remains stationary or steps back.
- ✕ The opponent defends.
- ---> Step back and strike the moment the opponent steps forward.
- --> Small step back and strike if the opponent remains stationary or steps forward.
- ⟶✕⟶ Step forward and strike the moment the opponent steps back defending.
- →✕ Step forward and strike if the opponent remains stationary or steps back while defending.
- -✕-> Step back and strike the moment the opponent steps forward while defending.
- ✕> Small step back and strike if the opponent remains stationary or steps forward.

NIDAN-WAZA

A. From *men* to *men*.

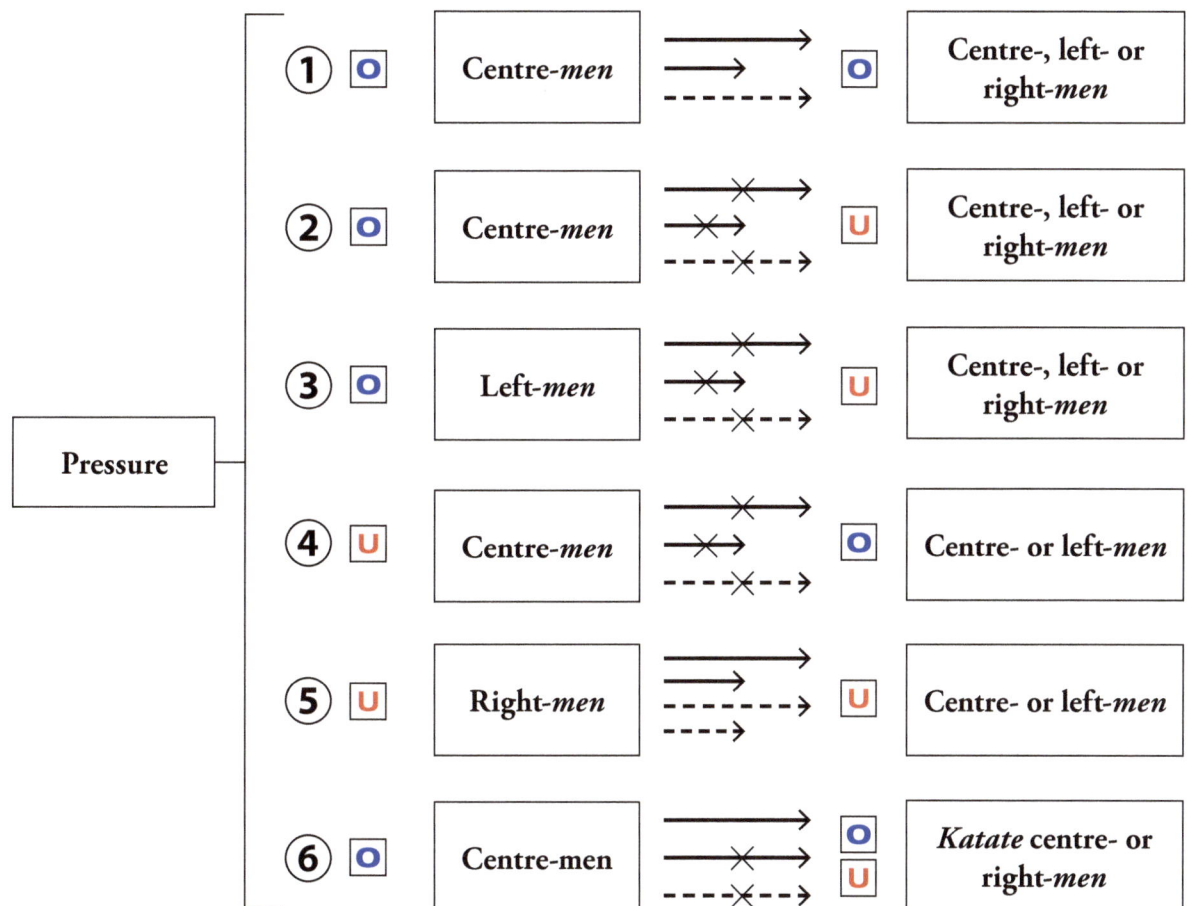

Note:

O (*omote*) The left-side of the (your) *shinai*.

U (*ura*) The right-side of the (your) *shinai*.

⟶ The moment the opponent steps back, step forward at the same speed and make a large strike.

→ When the opponent remains stationary, take a little step forward while executing a small, sharp strike.

--⟶ Keeping control of the centre, extend your left hand and strike the moment the opponent steps forward. After the strike, make sure that your posture is straight as you try to make yourself taller than the opponent.

--→ Step back and strike if the opponent remains stationary or if they take a small step forward.

✕ The opponent defends or parries.

The *motodachi* should allow an attack on their centre-*men* from the *omote* side, defend, and then receive the second attack from the *ura* side. This will enable the execution of correct *nidan-waza*.

A1: *Omote*-centre-*men* → *omote*-centre-*men*

A2: *Omote*-centre-*men* ⇹ *ura*-right-*men*

A3: *Ura*-right-*men* → *omote*-centre-*men*

Important Points

— When changing from *omote* to *ura* (or *ura* to *omote*) and the first strike is blocked, stop the attack, relax the shoulders and quickly move the left fist over the opponent's *shinai*, or use the right fist as a fulcrum while turning the wrists to change direction.

B. From *men* to *doh*.

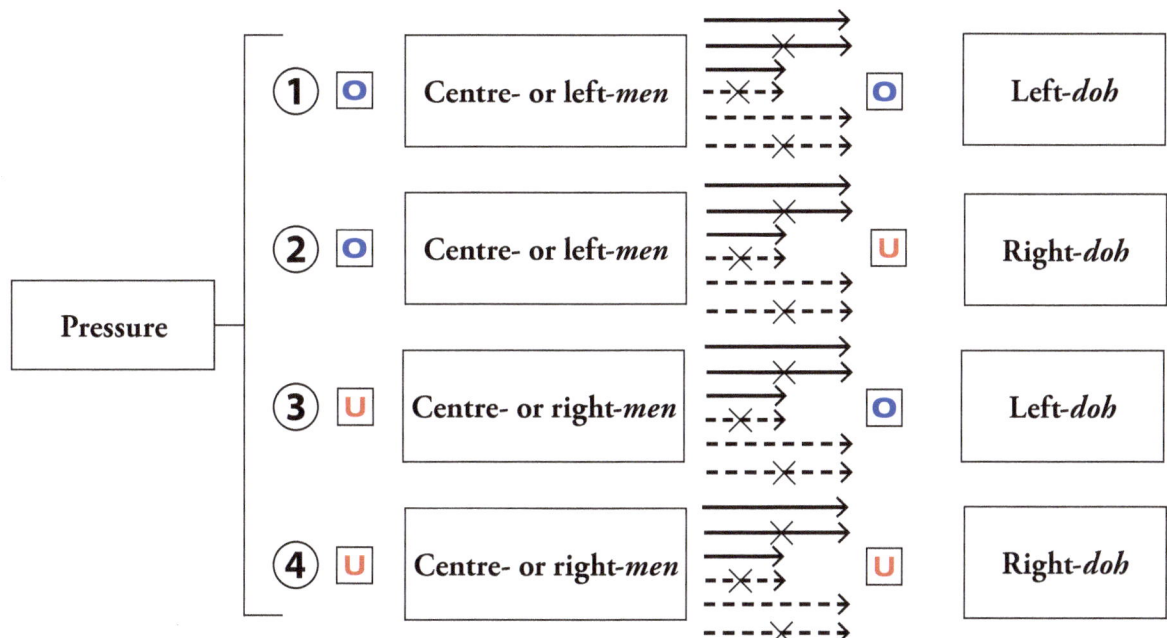

B2: *Omote*-centre-*men* → right-*doh*

B2: *Omote*-left-*men* —✕→ right-*doh*

B2: *Omote*-centre-*men* ----> right-*hiki*-*doh* (*hiki* = moving back)

B4: *Ura*-right-*men* ⟶ right-*doh*

Important Points

— There are three main types of *ashi-sabaki* to strike *left-doh*.
  1. Forward to the diagonal right from the right foot, strike, and then take a step back to the right.
  2. Forward to the diagonal left from the left foot and strike. Pass the opponent on the left-side.
  3. Forward to the diagonal left from the right foot and strike. Pass the opponent on the left-side.

— There are three main methods of *ashi-sabaki* to strike *right-doh*:
  1. Forward from the right foot to the right side and strike. Pass the opponent on the right-side.
  2. Forward from the right foot to the left side and strike. Pass the opponent on the left-side.
  3. Forward from the left foot to the left side and strike. Pass the opponent on the left-side.

— *Motodachi* should do the following when receiving right-*doh* in the case of techniques 1 and 2:
  1. Big step back and to the side from the right foot as the attacker moves forward to strike.
  2. Big step forward from the left foot and to the side when the attacker is moving back to strike (*hiki-waza*). It is important that the opponent sufficiently extends their strikes and moves straight and quickly.

— After moving to the side, *motodachi* should make a half-turn on the spot and strike *men*. Or, the moment the opponent moves back, advance from the right foot and strike *men*. *Motodachi* should practise striking *men* at the same time.

— Try moving in various directions. For example, to the diagonal right and strike the opponent's left-*men*; turn the wrists and strike right-*doh*; advance to the diagonal right and strike right-*men*; or move back to the diagonal left and strike right-*doh*. Try to strike freely from whatever position you are in.

C. From *men* to *kote*.

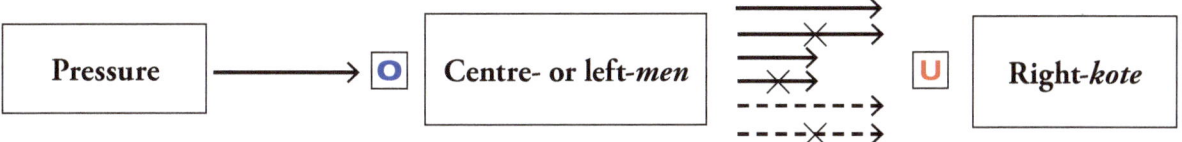

C: *Omote*-centre-*men* ⤳ *ura kote*

C: *Omote*-centre-*men* → *katsugi-kote* (*katsugi* = *shinai* over the left shoulder)

Important Points

— Pressure the opponent by taking a big step forward and strike centre-*men* or left-*men* from the *omote* side, then quickly return the *shinai* over the centreline and strike *kote*.
— If striking *kote* while retreating, move back to the diagonal right as the strike is made.
— Always strike *kote* without delay after creating an opening through hitting centre- or right-*men* from the *omote* side.

D. From *kote* to *men*, *doh* or *kote*.

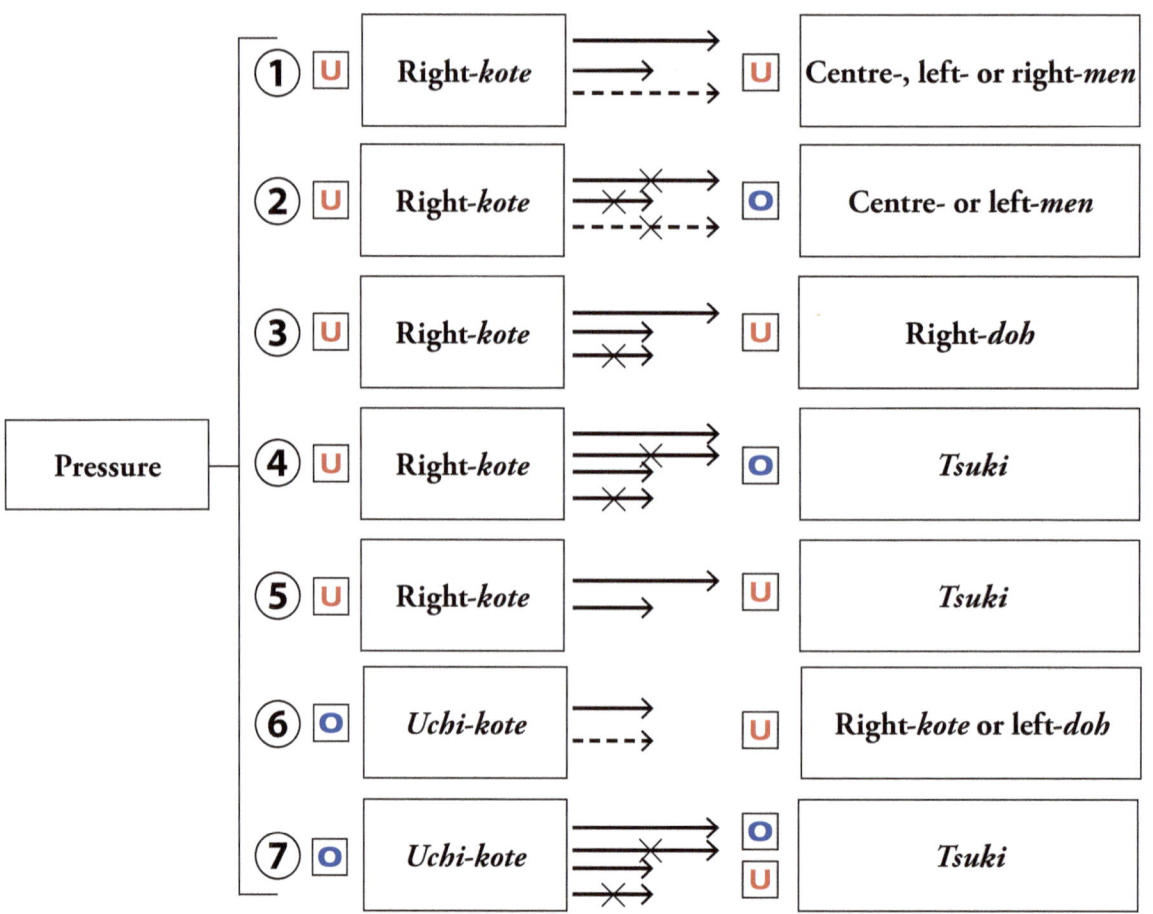

D1: *Ura*-right-*kote* ⟶ *ura*-centre-*men*

D2: *Ura*-right-*kote* ⟶×⟶ *omote*-centre-*men*   Variation

D3: *Ura*-right-*kote* ⟶ *ura*-right-*doh*

Important Points

— With a right-*kote* attack, if the opponent is shorter or the *shinai* is lower, move the *shinai* along the top of theirs and strike. If the opponent is taller, move the *shinai* under the opponent's. To strike right-*kote*, the right foot is moved slightly to the diagonal left to cut across the opponent's centreline.

— When striking *uchi-kote* (*kote* strike from the inside, i.e., from the left side of the opponent's *shinai* as opposed to the right), step diagonally forward with the right foot, change the cutting angle to the diagonal right, and strike down diagonally from above. Immediately return the right foot over the centreline and strike the opponent's right-*kote* on the *ura* side.

E. From *doh* to *men* or *doh*.

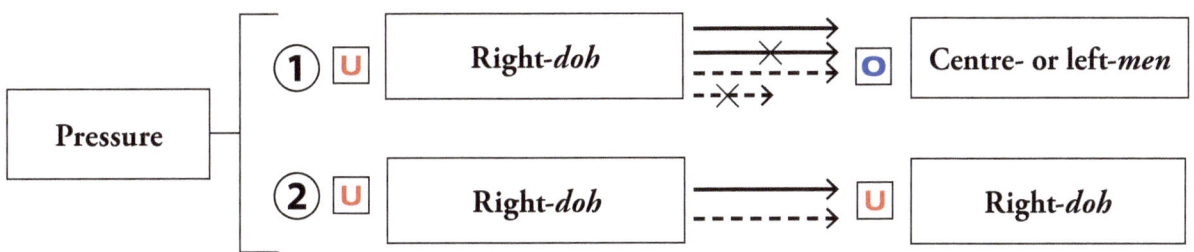

E1: *Ura*-right-*doh* ⟶ *omote*-centre-*men*

E1: *Ura*-right-*doh*   ---> *omote*-centre-*men*

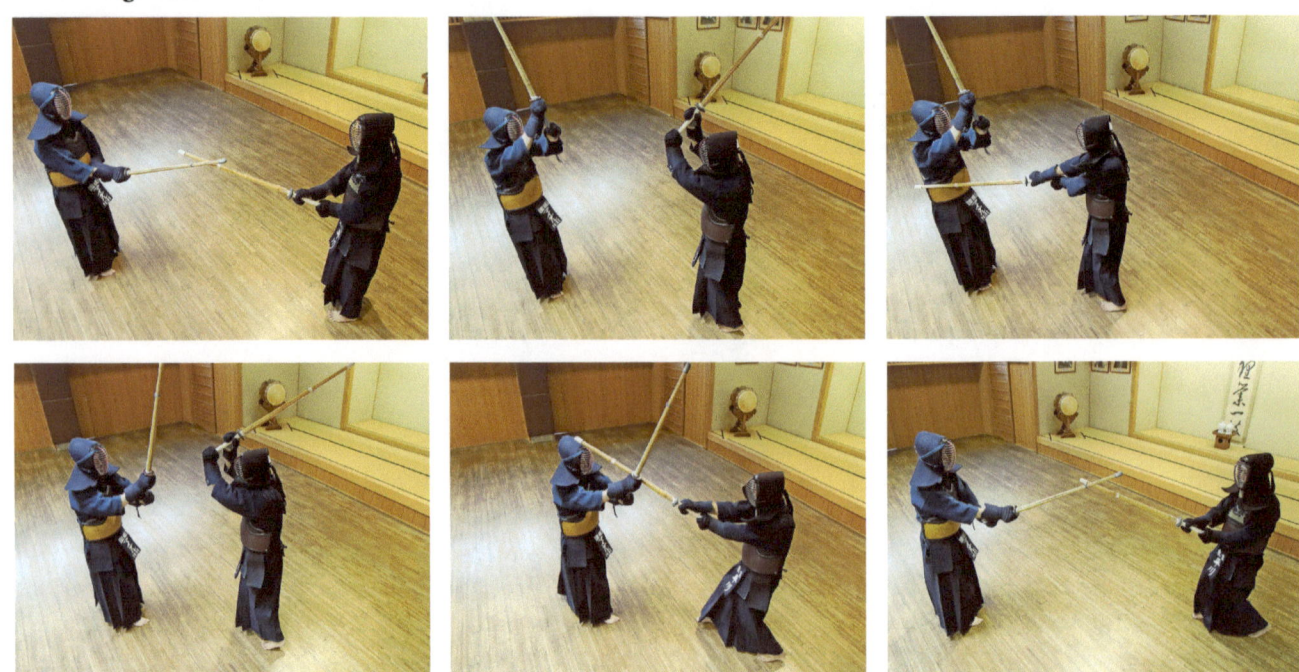

Important Points

- To receive right-*doh*, *motodachi* should take a large step back from the right foot and turn to the side. Take a big step back from the left foot to receive the *men* strike. Then, without breaking posture, *motodachi* should retreat in a straight line while extending both arms. Allow the right-*doh* to be struck and then take another large step back and allow another strike to right-*doh*.
- There are few opportunities to make consecutive strikes to right-*doh*. After hitting right-*doh* the first time, pressure the opponent by starting to strike either centre- or left-*men*. Stop just before making contact and quickly strike right-*doh* again.
- Raise the *shinai* overhead and kick off with the right foot to strike centre- or left-*men* on the *omote* side while moving back after striking right-*doh*.

Shin-ki-ryoku-itchi

Chiba Shusaku of the Hokushin Itto-ryu school of swordsmanship said the following of "*shin-ki-ryoku-itchi*". "*Shin*" (mind) refers to the static action of the mind that deals with perception and judgment. "*Ki*" (outward action based upon the judgment of the mind) is the dynamic function of the mind that is the intent borne by the perception and judgment of the mind. "*Ryoku*" is the physical action of the body, or technique. When the mind perceives the opponent's movements, and then decides to attack, this will not result in a consolidated strike. It is important that before executing a technique, your mind (*shin*), energy (*ki*) and techniques (*ryoku*) are already in unison.

F. From *tsuki* to *men*, *doh* or *kote*.

Pressure

① O *Tsuki* → O Centre-, left-, right- or *katate-men*

② O *Tsuki* → U Centre-, right- or *katate-men*

③ O *Tsuki* → O Left-*doh*

④ O *Tsuki* → U Right-*kote* or *tsuki*

⑤ U *Tsuki* → U Centre- or right-*men*

⑥ U *Tsuki* → O Centre- or left-*men*, or *tsuki*

⑦ U *Tsuki* → U Right-*doh*

⑧ U *Tsuki* → U Right-*kote*

F1: *Omote-katate-tsuki* → *omote*-centre-*men*

F2: *Omote-morote-tsuki* ⟶ *ura*-katate-centre-*men*

F4: *Omote-katate-tsuki* ⟶ *ura*-right-*kote*

F7: *Ura-katate-tsuki* ⟶ *ura*-right-*doh*

Important Points

— The movement of the *shinai* tip is very direct and fast with *tsuki*. This scares the opponent and creates an opening to strike. It can also force the opponent to step back, creating the ideal distance from which a strike can be made. However, because the movement is small, it is easy for the opponent to dodge and defend. Therefore, it is important that *tsuki* be executed without fear of losing, with full spirit, and by using the hips.

— *Tsuki-waza* can be done from both the *omote* and *ura* sides. It can also be executed with one (*katate*) or both hands (*morote*), so both methods should be studied.

— Practise *tsuki* with different types of body movements and combined with various *shikake-waza*. For example, execute a *tsuki* from the *omote* side. The moment the opponent defends, try *suriage-waza* or *hari-waza* from the *ura* side and strike either *men* or right-*doh*.

SANDAN-WAZA (renzoku-waza)

The following types of *sandan-waza* (*renzoku-waza*) will be examined in the diagrams below:
A. From *men* to *men, doh, kote* or *tsuki*
B. From *men-doh* to *men, doh, kote* or *tsuki*
C. From *men-kote* to *men, doh, kote* or *tsuki*
D. From *kote-men* to *men, doh, kote* or *tsuki*
E. From *tsuki-men* to *men, doh, kote* or *tsuki*
F. From *tsuki-doh* to *men, doh, kote* or *tsuki*
G. From *tsuki-kote* to *men, kote* or *tsuki*
H. From *tsuki-tsuki* to *men, doh, kote* or *tsuki*

A. From *men-men* to *men, doh, kote* or *tsuki*.

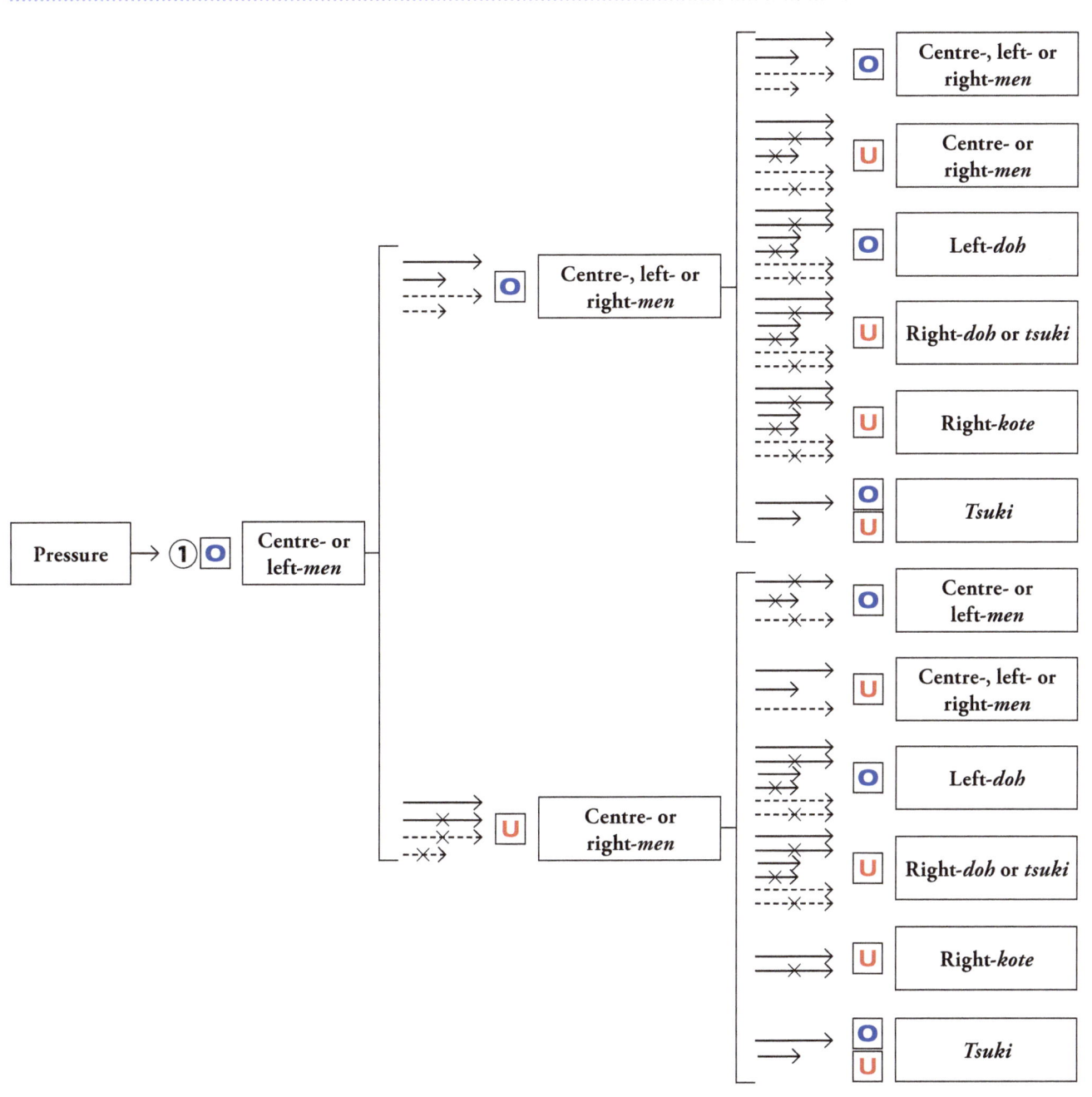

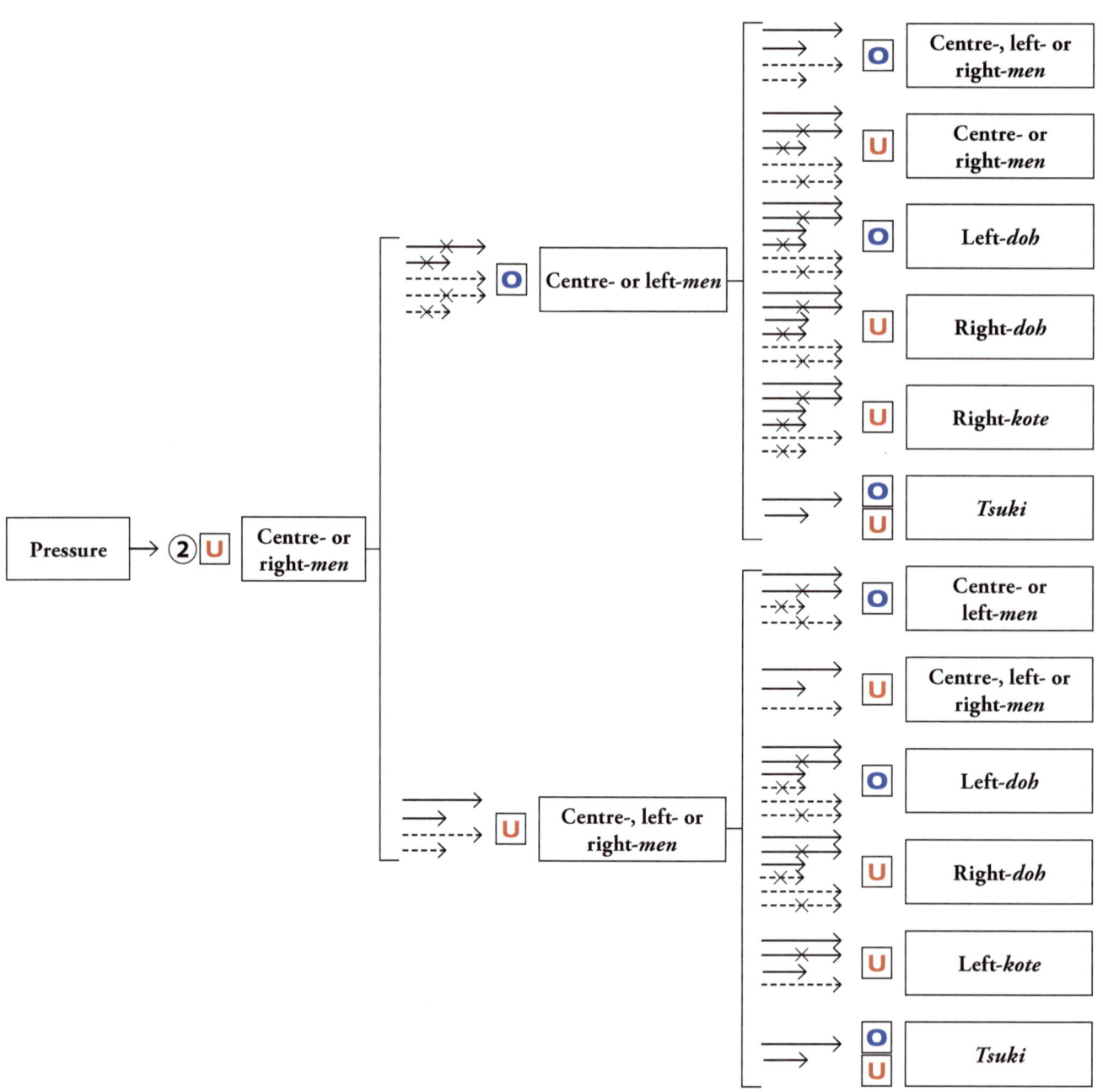

B. From *men-doh* to *men*, *doh*, *kote* or *tsuki*.

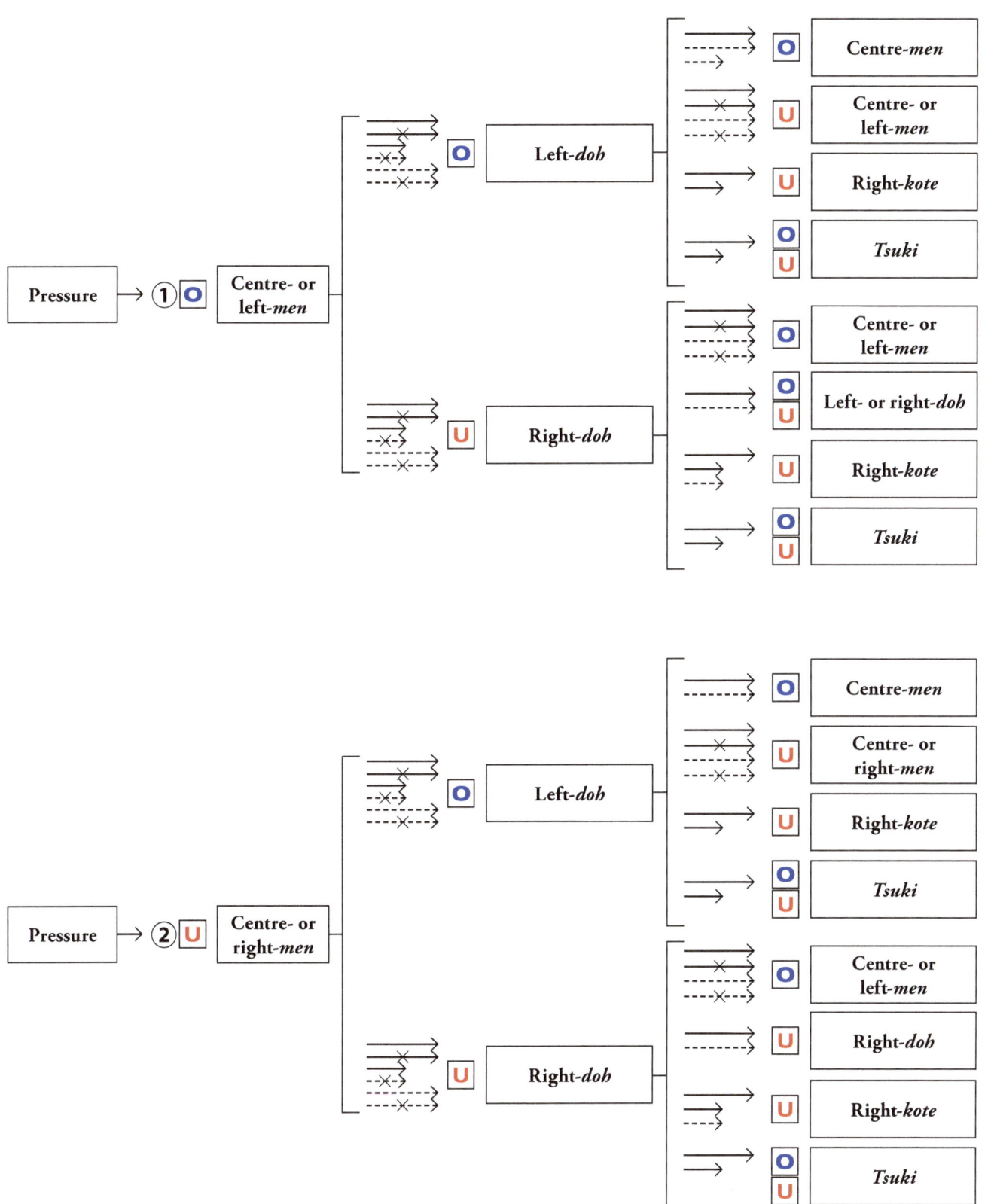

C. From *men-kote* to *men*, *doh*, *kote* or *tsuki*.

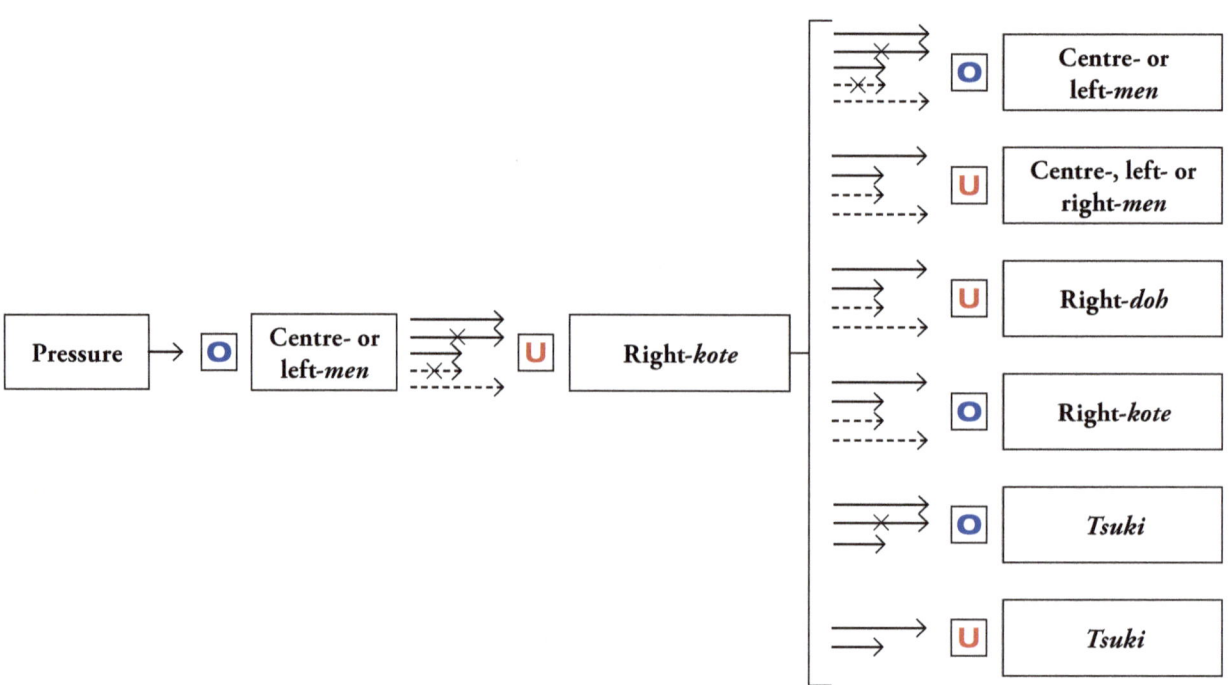

The movement of the *kensen* (*shinai* tip)

If you have the feeling of pressing down on the opponent's fist with the tip of your *shinai*, you will kill the opponent's *kensen*. Proceed with the feeling of breaking the opponent's *kamae*. Pressurise your opponent and disarm them mentally. If you must move back, do so as if concealing your body behind the tip of your *shinai* so that you can defend resolutely. It is essential that pressure is kept on the opponent.

In the Itto-ryu school of swordsmanship, it was said that the *kensen* should undulate like small ripples on water, or like a wagtail bird's tail bobbing up and down so that the opponent cannot judge when you are going to unleash an attack. At the same time, one's intent to attack should manifest in your *kensen* to pressurise the opponent.

The Munen-ryu school teaches keeping the tip of the sword still and pressing the opponent with a steadfast mind, striking the instant an opening is revealed. There are several different ways to do this, but the *kensen* can decide the opponent's fate. Also, without severing the connection with the opponent's *shinai* tip, as if they are joined by a thread, move forward when they move back and vice versa to maintain the same distance. This will provide opportunities to capitalise on.

D. From *kote-men* to *men*, *doh*, *kote* or *tsuki*.

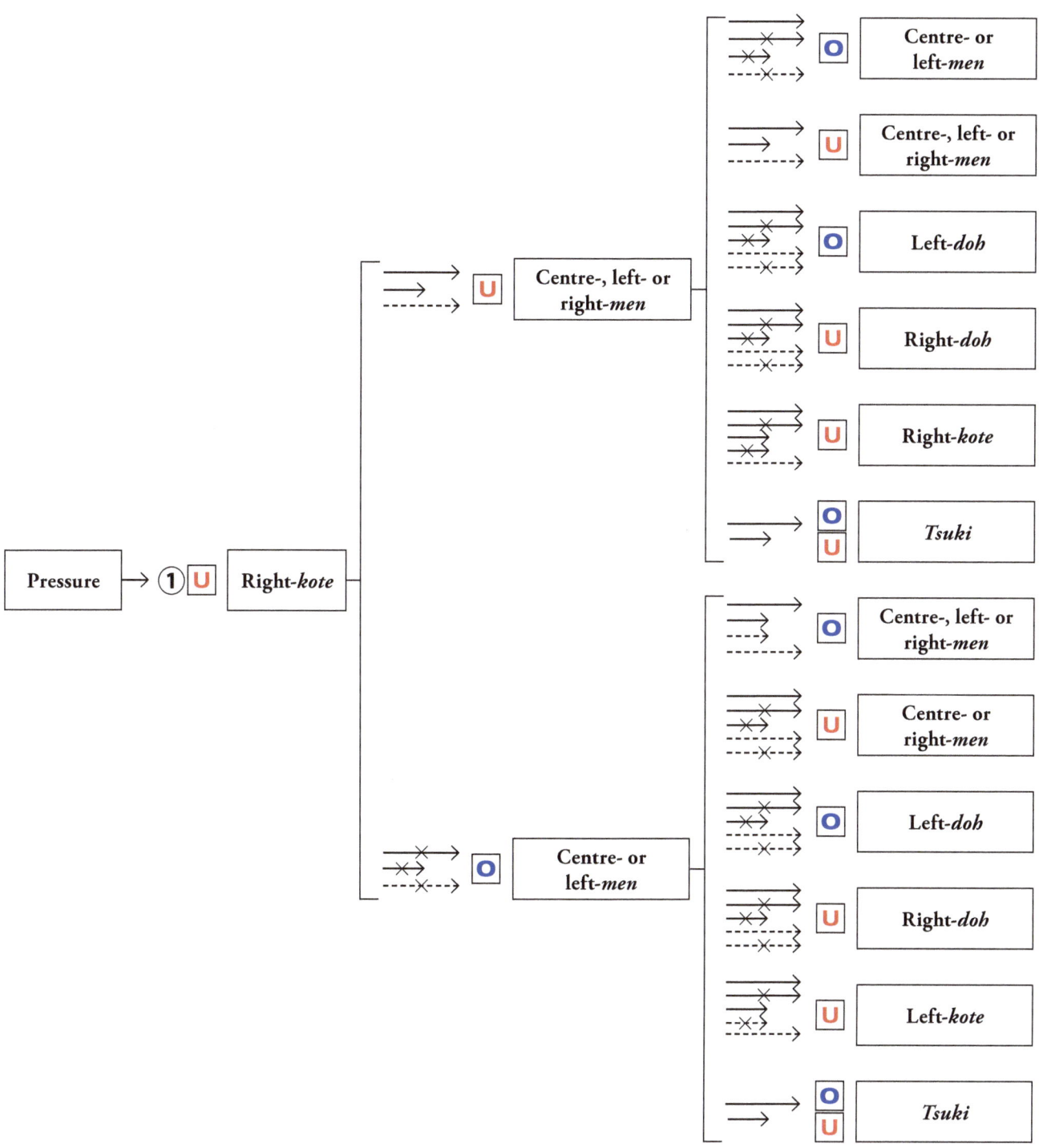

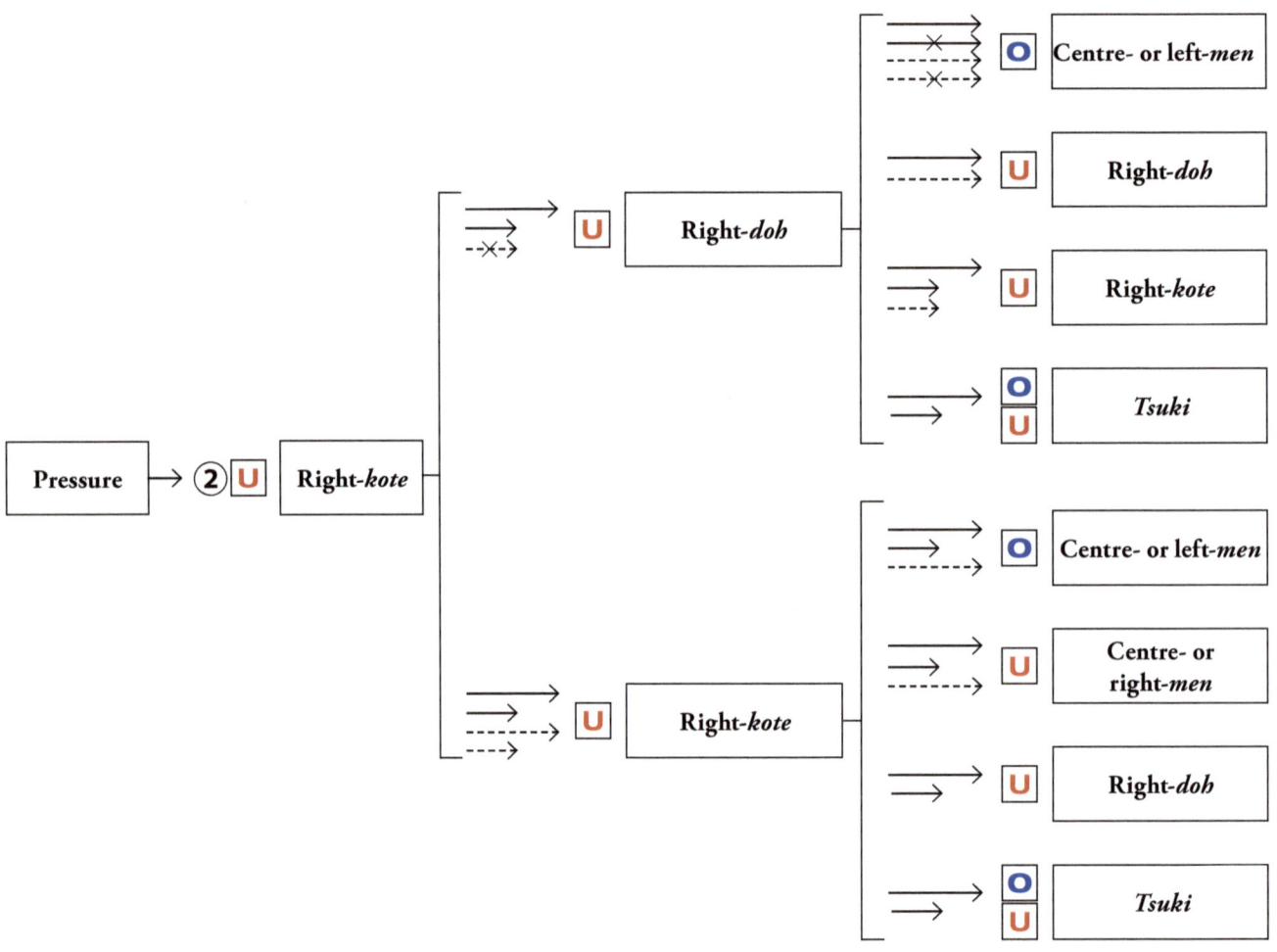

> **Kakegoe (vocalisation, usually a shout)**
>
> *Kakegoe* focuses the spirit, concentrates the power of the mind and body giving power to the *shinai* as it strikes. It can also intimidate the opponent and stifle their movements. *Kakegoe* needs to be natural and powerful, and fit with your movement. Avoid *kakegoe* that is contrived. There are three ways in which *kakegoe* can be used to your advantage:
> 1. Shout to win. After striking, shout loudly to make the opponent unable to respond.
> 2. Shout when pressuring your opponent to confuse them. Attack the moment they start an ill-prepared movement.
> 3. When under pressure, look carefully for the moment your opponent tries to make a strike and immediately make a loud scream. The opponent will be unsure of your intentions and become confused. Strike that moment to win.

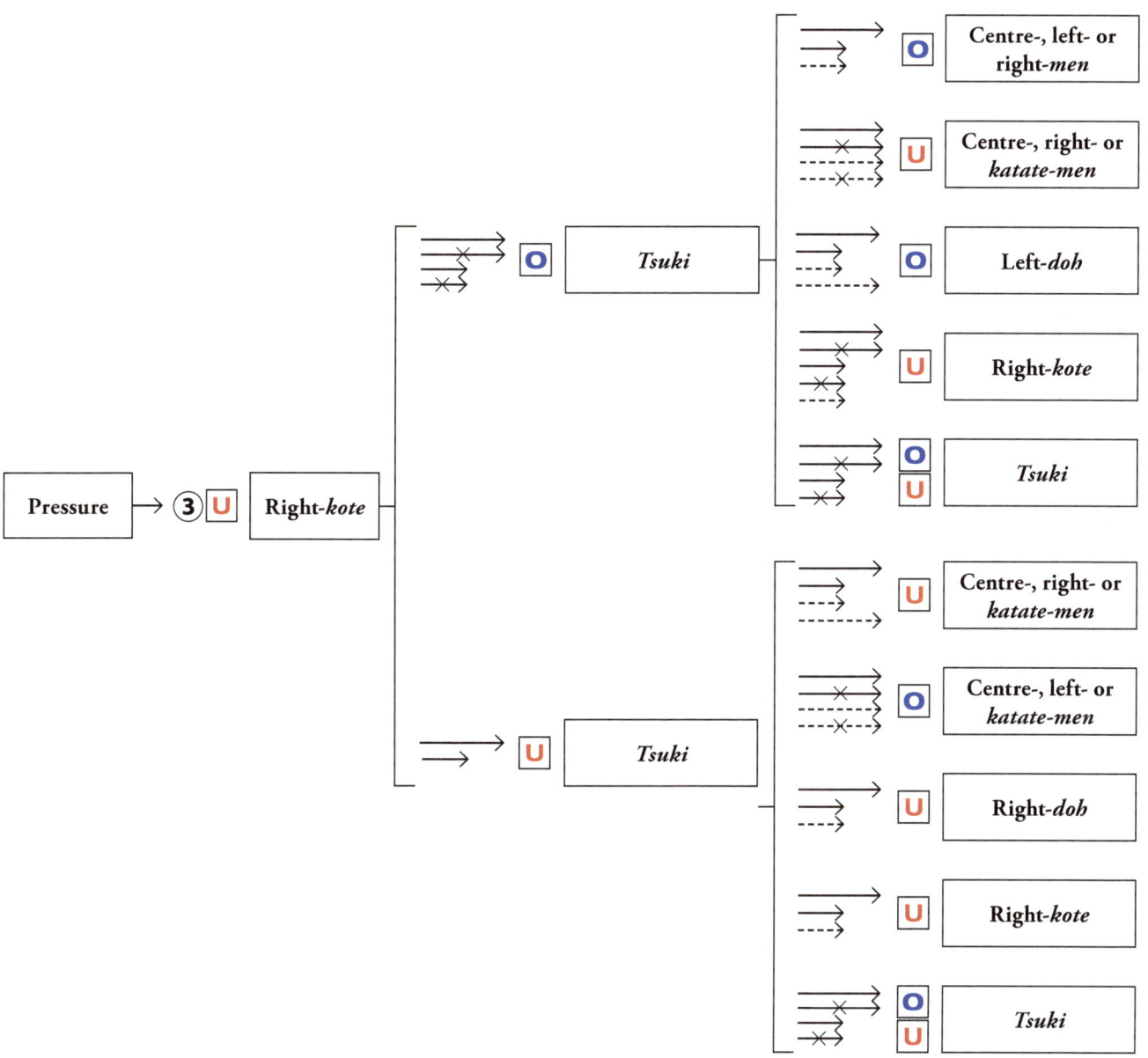

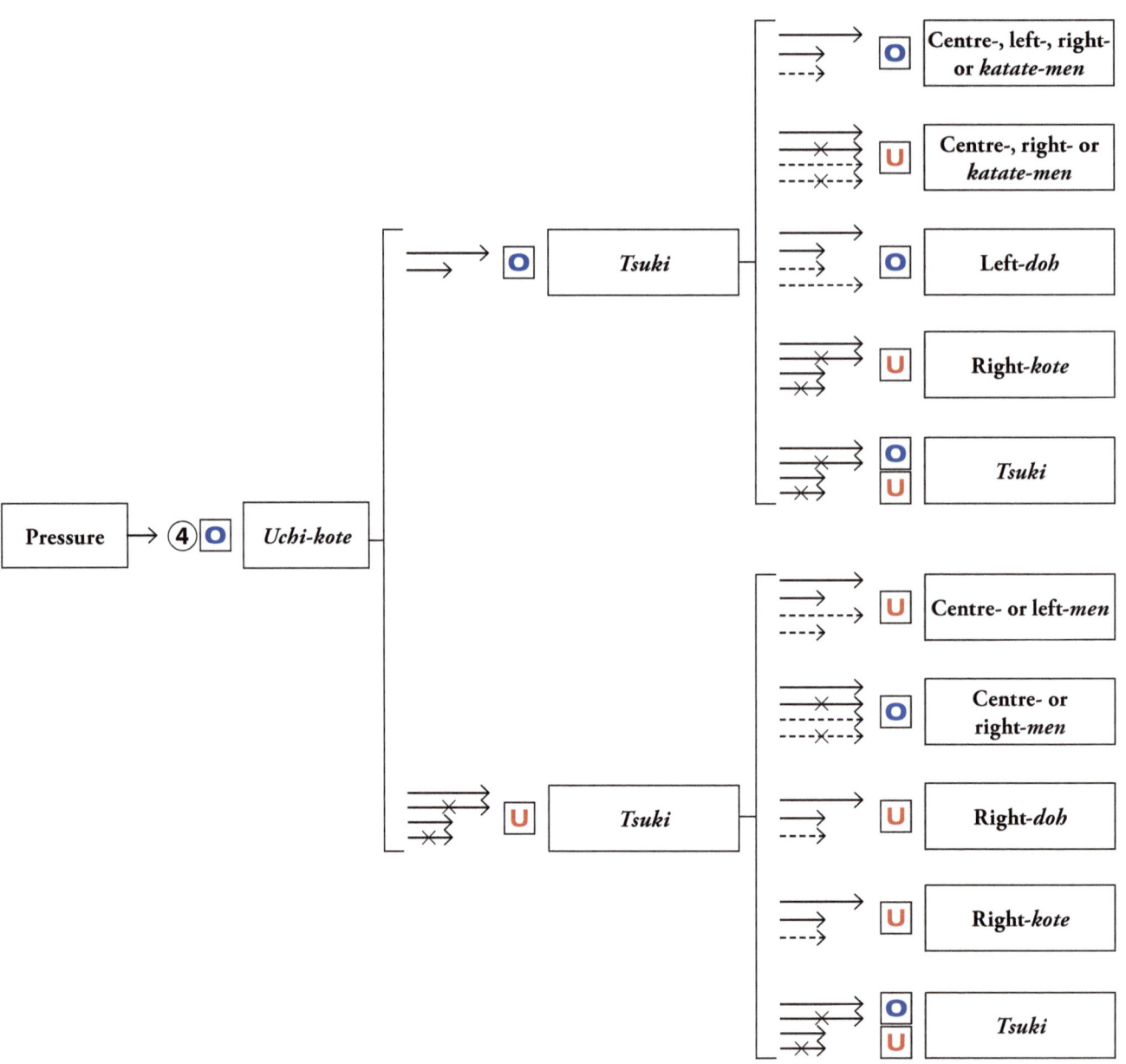

E. From *tsuki-men* to *men*, *doh*, *kote* or *tsuki*.

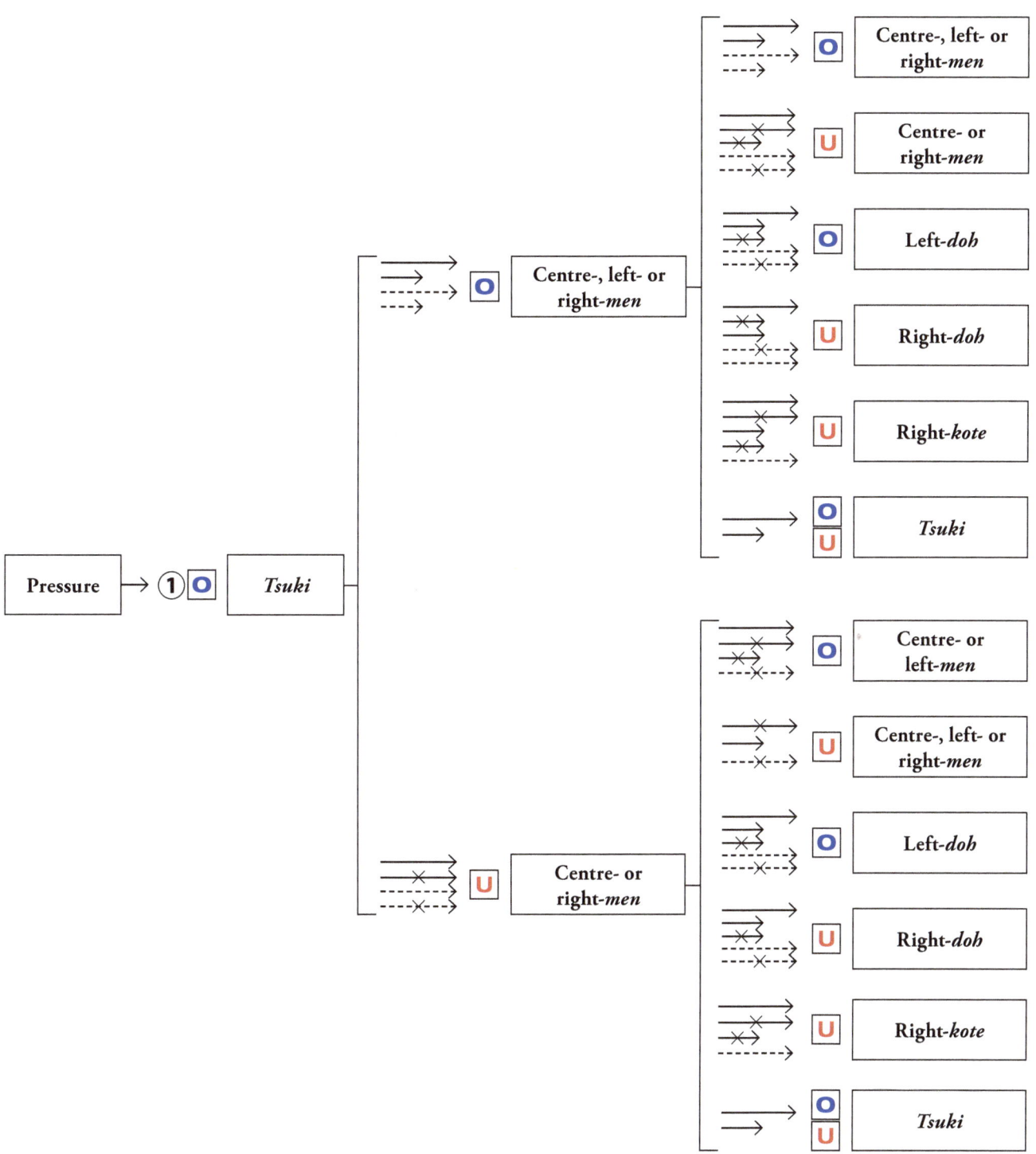

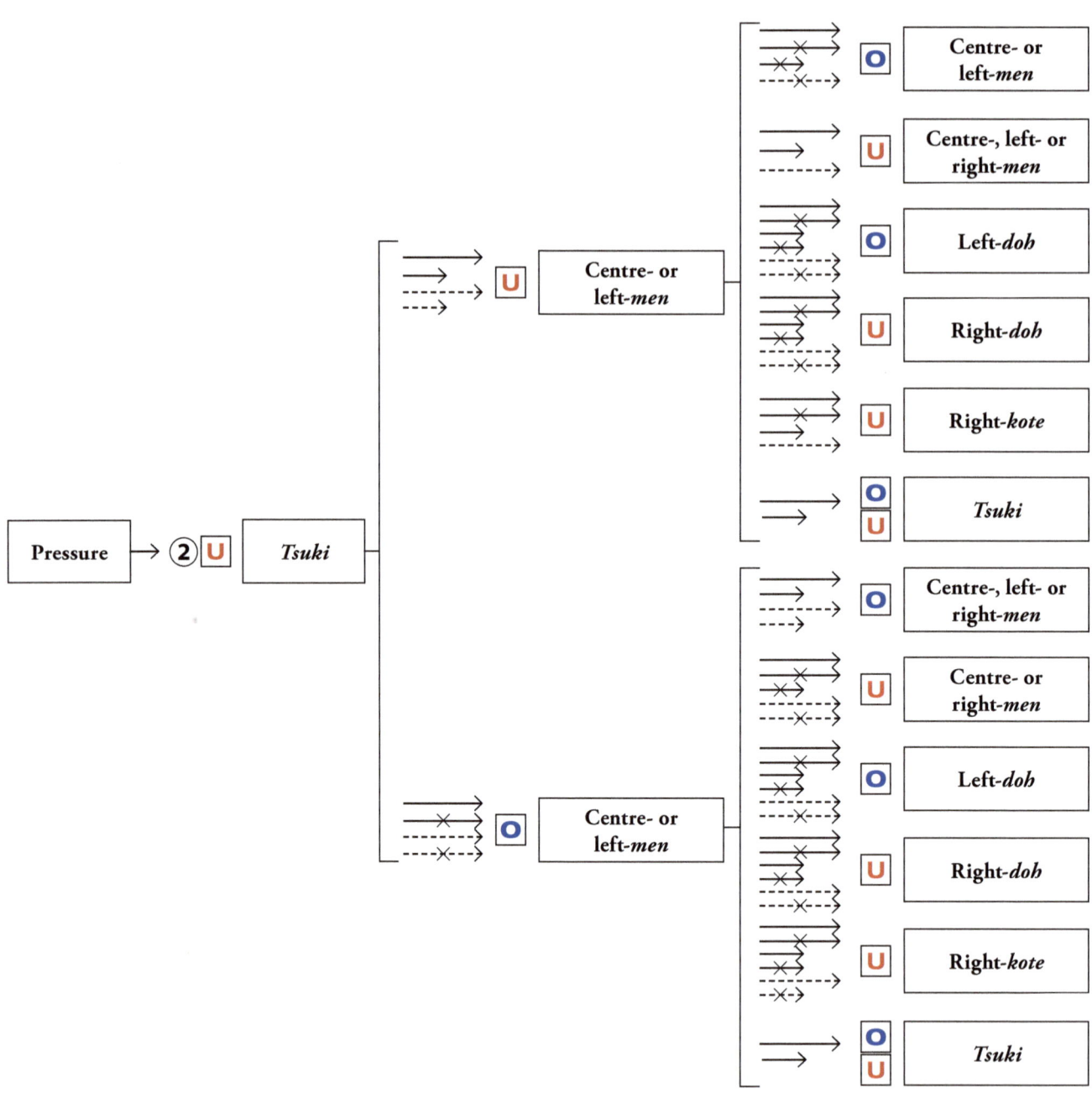

F. From *tsuki-doh* to *men*, *doh*, *kote* or *tsuki*.

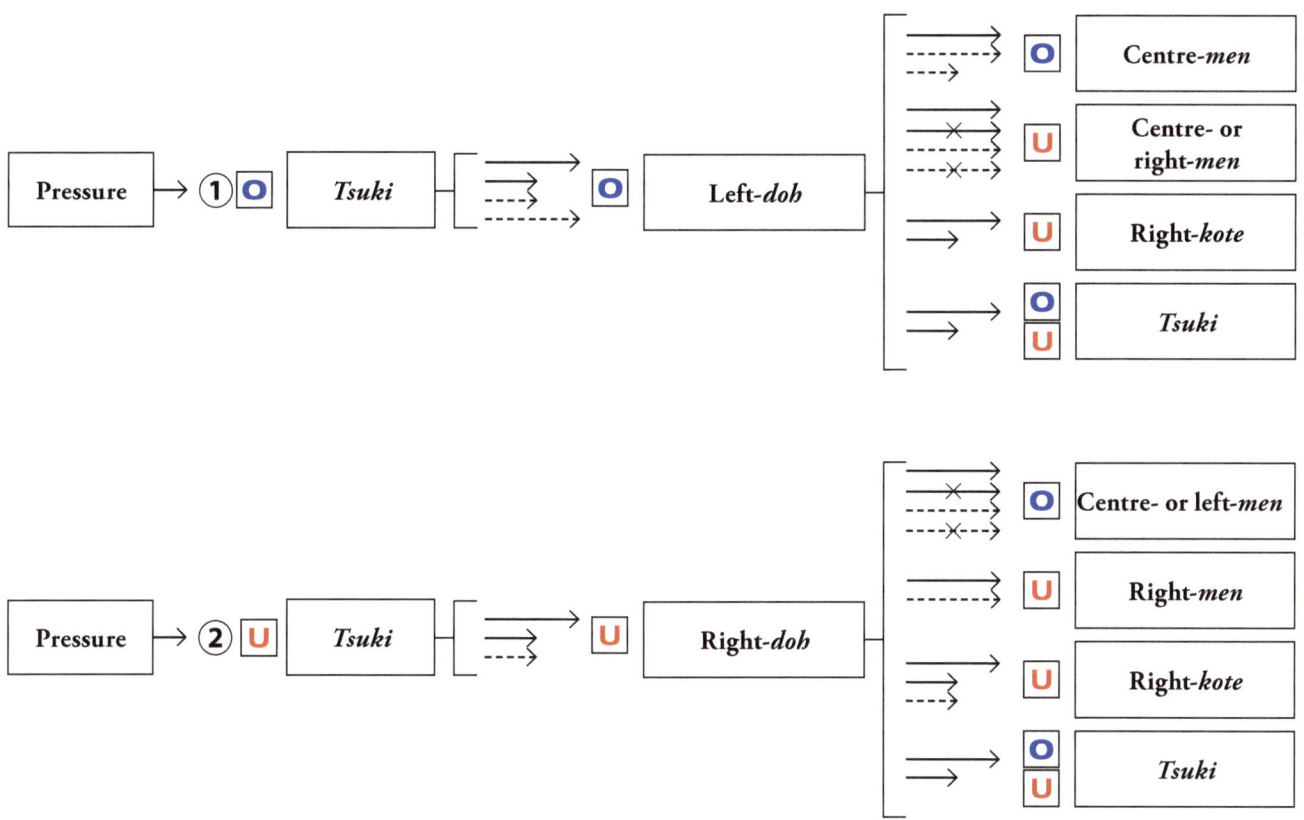

> **Kyo-jitsu (falsehood and truth)**
>
> *Kyo* refers to emptiness and is a state with an absence of mental strength and energy. Conversely, *jitsu* is a state of replete spirit and with no openings or negligence. *Jitsu* is the position of victory, and *kyo* is that of defeat. Therefore, with *jitsu* it is important to strike *kyo*, at the same time as showing *kyo* to your opponent to make them think that they can take advantage of the situation and strike. Within *jitsu* there is *kyo*, and within *kyo* there is *jitsu*, so it can be said that *kyo* and *jitsu* are one. It is necessary to be able to change depending on the situation in order to win.

G. From *tsuki-kote* to *men*, *kote* or *tsuki*.

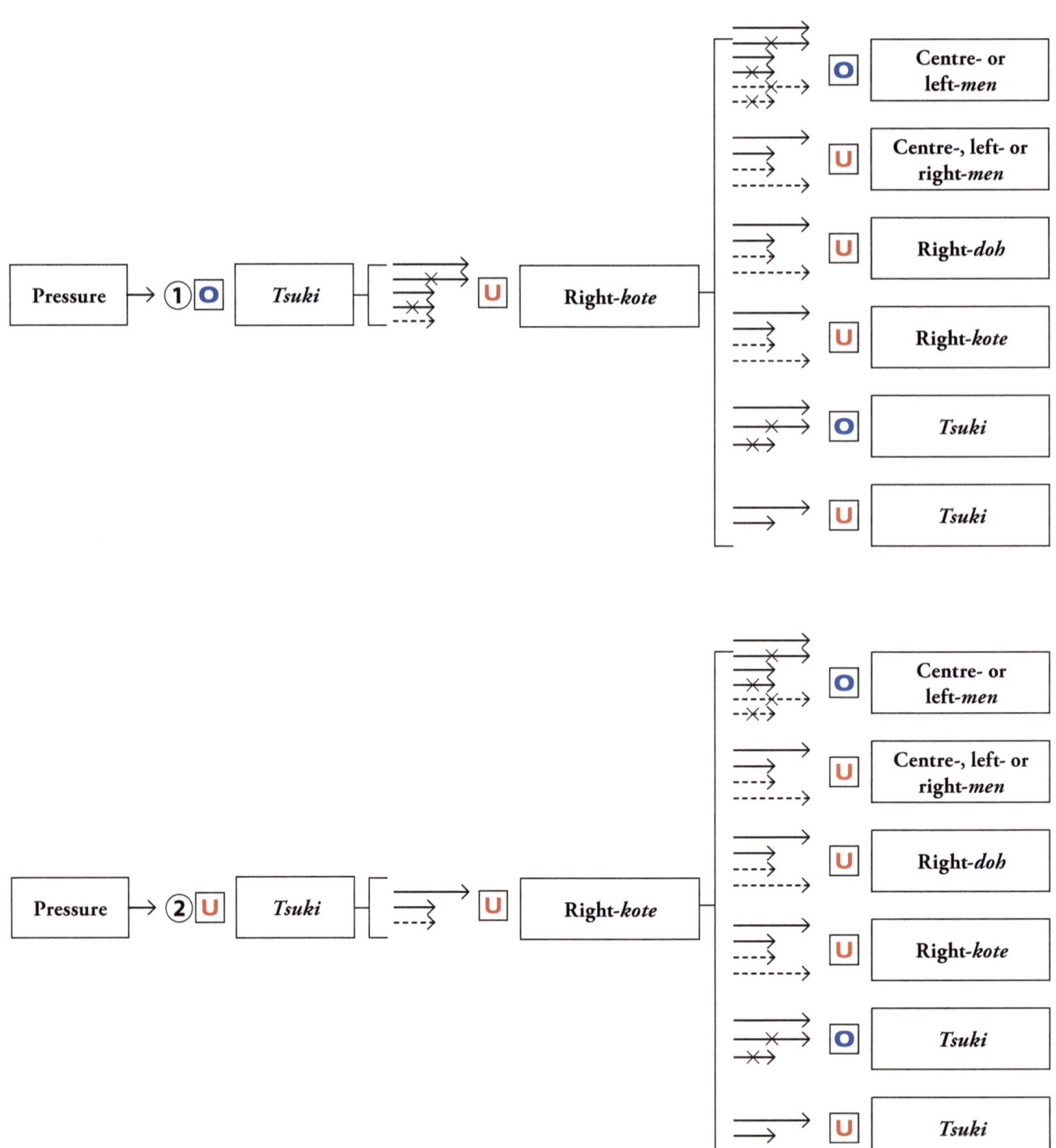

H. From *tsuki-tsuki* to *men, doh, kote* or *tsuki*.

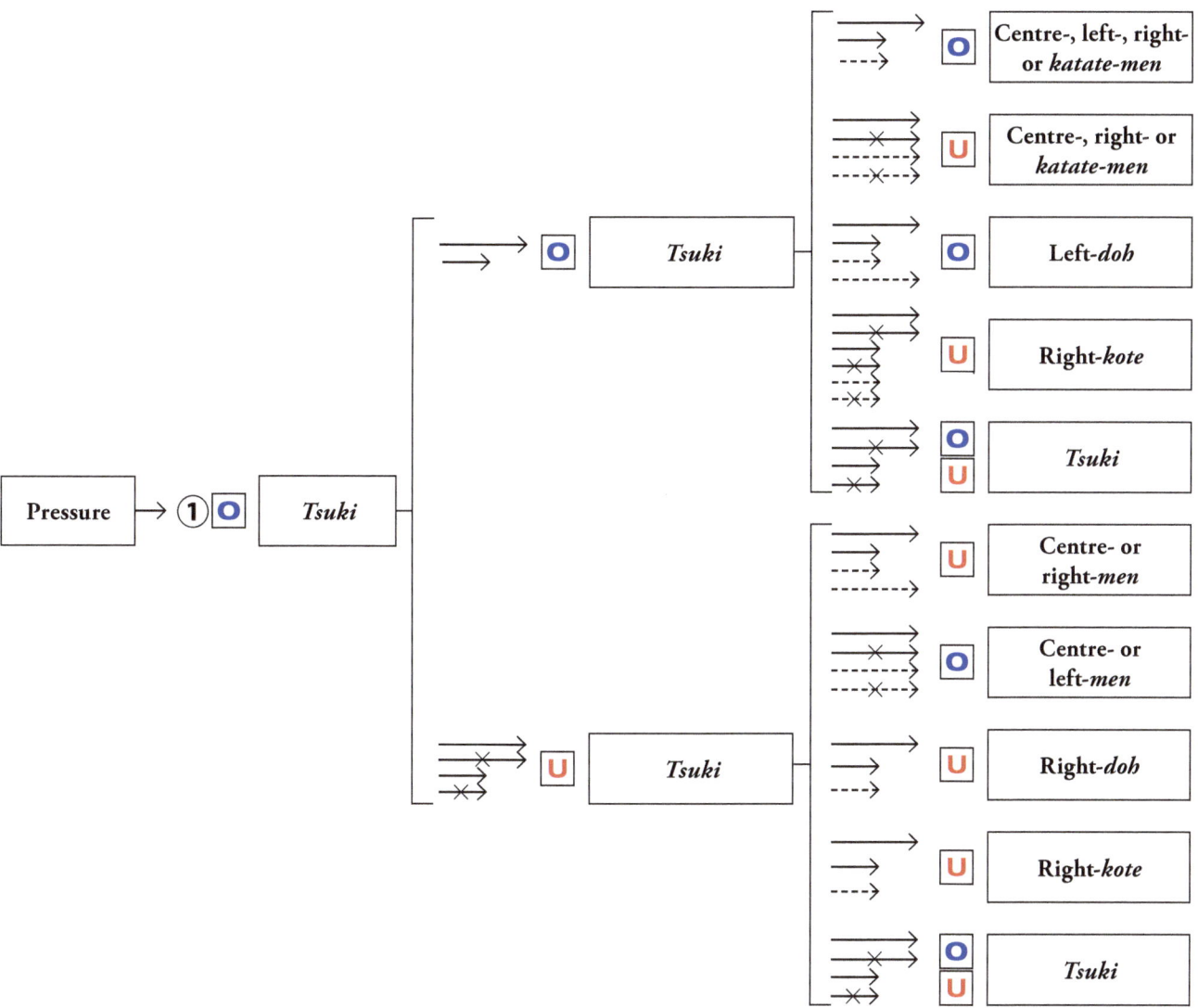

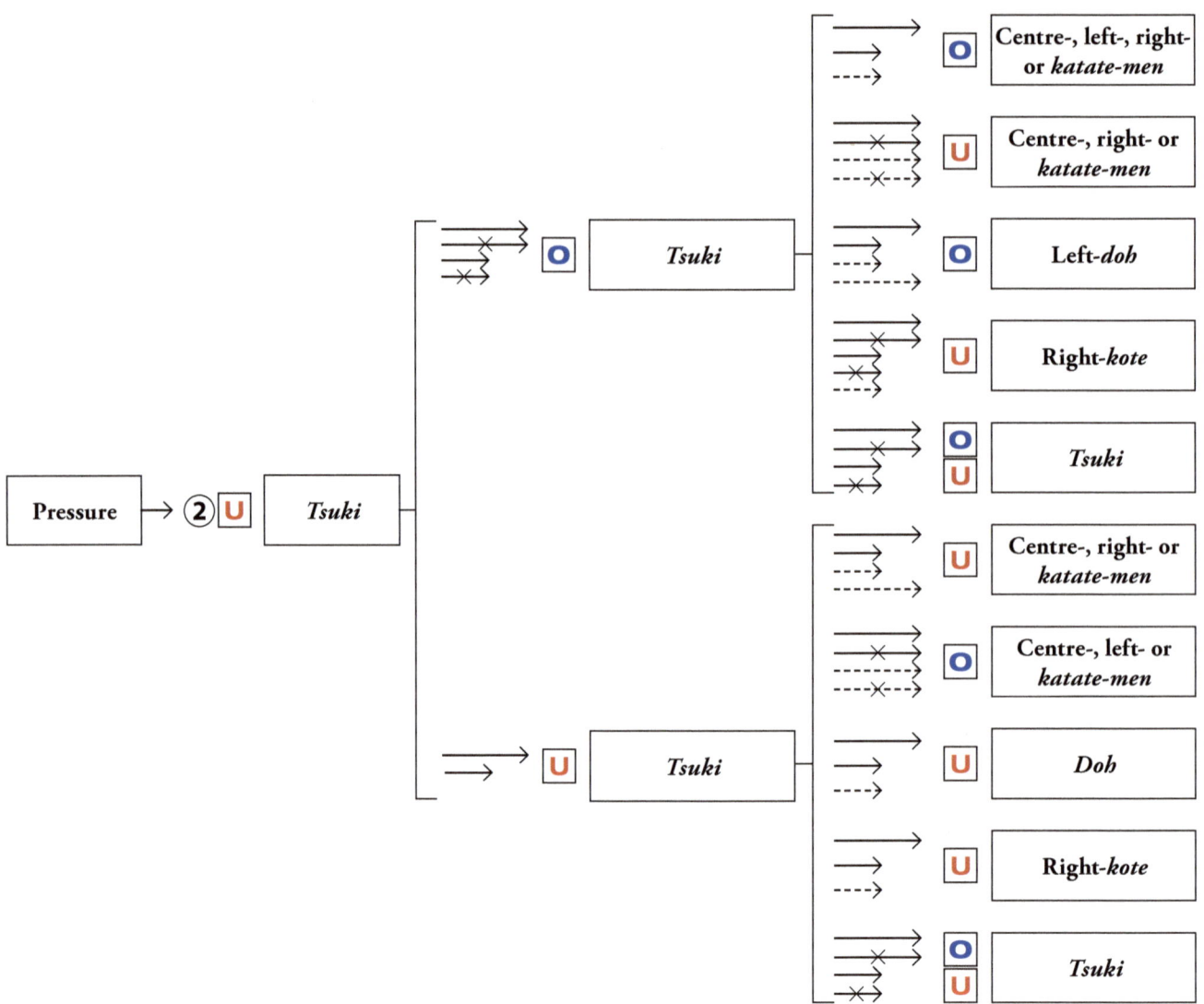

Important Points

— When executing *renzoku-waza*, the finishing technique becomes more complicated depending on whether the opponent defends, attacks, or moves when pressured.
— It is important to practise pressuring the opponent by using the wrists to change direction from the *omote* side to the *ura* side.
— Depending on the opponent's movements, maintain an interval from which a correct strike can be made. Move forward and back quickly without breaking your posture.
— Once you can move forward and backward effectively, practise moving to the left, right, and diagonally before striking.
— In response to pressure from the opponent, the *motodachi* should not just move back or forward, but also to the left and right, as well as diagonally. These changes are necessary so that the attacker can learn to strike *renzoku-waza* from all directions.
— Because it is easy for the opponent to defend or counter when pressured with the same rhythm, alternate the timing, and change between small and big techniques.
— *Sandan-waza* and *renzoku-waza* are complicated because you never know how your opponent will respond. You will need to pre-empt their reaction. Try to make your own combinations, and practise striking from every direction – *omote*, *ura*, above, below, left, right. Find your own special technique.

Sandan-waza (renzoku-waza) examples

Example 1

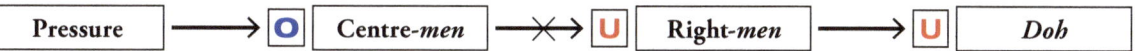

Pressure the opponent and strike *men* from the *omote* side. If the opponent steps back to defend, change to the *ura* side and strike diagonal right-*men*. If the opponent remains stationary or steps back, move forward and strike right-*doh*. In the case of *sandan-waza*, if the interval is too close after striking right-*men* from the *ura* side, practise adding *taiatari* (bodycheck) and then striking *doh*.

Example 2

Pressure the opponent and strike diagonal right-*men* from the *ura* side. If the opponent remains in the same place or takes a small step forward to defend, step back and strike *men*. The moment the opponent steps back, advance and strike *men*. After striking the second centre-*men* in *nidan-waza*, move forward again and strike *men* once more.

Example 3

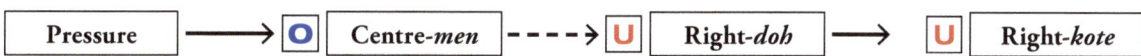

Pressure the opponent and strike *men* from the *omote* side. If the opponent steps forward, strike *doh* form the *ura* side by stepping back. If the opponent then remains stationary or retreats slightly, move forward and strike *kote* from the *ura* side. With *nidan-waza*, after striking centre-*men*, use *harai-waza* and strike the opponent's right-*doh* while moving back (*hiki-doh*). In *sandan-waza*, try adding *hari-waza* and then striking right-*kote* etc.

Example 4

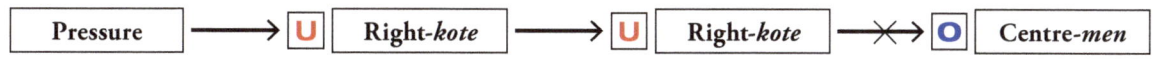

Pressure the opponent. If they remain stationary or take a step back, strike right-*kote* twice with small strikes. The moment the opponent steps back to defend, step in and execute a big *men* strike. It is important to change the striking rhythm to small-small-big. When pressuring with the first right-*kote* strike, push down (*osae*) on the opponent's *shinai* and move the body forward to the diagonal right. Then return to the centreline and strike right-*kote* again. Also, you can use *harai-waza* to strike right-*kote*. The moment the opponent defends, change to the *omote* side and strike *men*.

Example 5

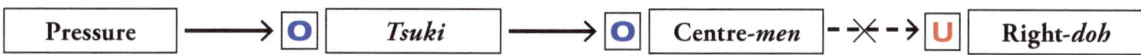

Pressure the opponent and execute *tsuki* (*katate* or *morote*) from the *omote* side. The moment the opponent takes a step back, move in and strike centre-*men*. As the opponent steps forward in response, step back and strike right-*doh*. When moving from *omote tsuki* to striking centre-*men*, do a big *harai* and step backward while striking right-*doh* if the opponent advances. Coax *motodachi* into striking to provide opportunities for *kaeshi-waza* as well.

Practising *sandan-waza* (*renzoku-waza*) with more than one *motodachi*

Try training with two, three or more *motodachi* at the same time. Manoeuvre smoothly and execute various techniques in succession, thinking about when to strike from *omote* or *ura*. Also try to work out changing the rhythm of strikes.

Key to diagrams

⟶ big and correct   → small and fast   --→ backward (*hiki-waza*)
● attacker   ①②③ *motodachi*

Example 1

Against two *motodachi*, stand in *chudan* at the distant interval of *toma*. Strikes should be big and precise. (examples C to E should be done small and correctly)

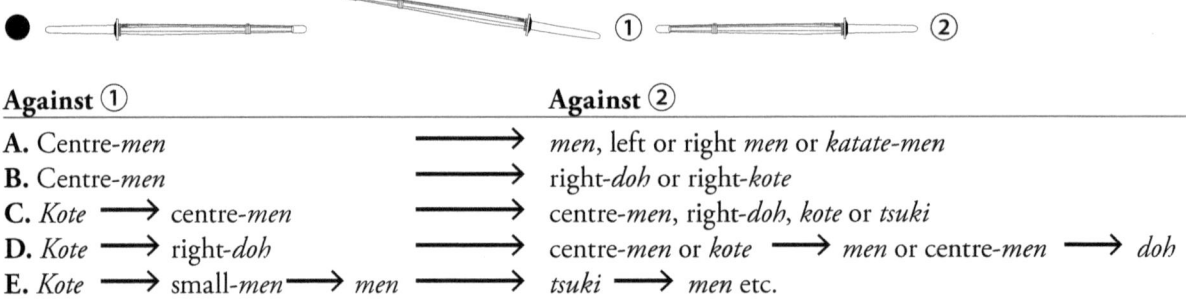

Against ①		Against ②
A. Centre-*men*	⟶	*men*, left or right *men* or *katate-men*
B. Centre-*men*	⟶	right-*doh* or right-*kote*
C. *Kote* ⟶ centre-*men*	⟶	centre-*men*, right-*doh*, *kote* or *tsuki*
D. *Kote* ⟶ right-*doh*	⟶	centre-*men* or *kote* ⟶ *men* or centre-*men* ⟶ *doh*
E. *Kote* ⟶ small-*men* ⟶ *men*	⟶	*tsuki* ⟶ *men* etc.

Example 2

The *maai* is at the closer *chikama* interval. The striker must think about the distance and strike in one movement.

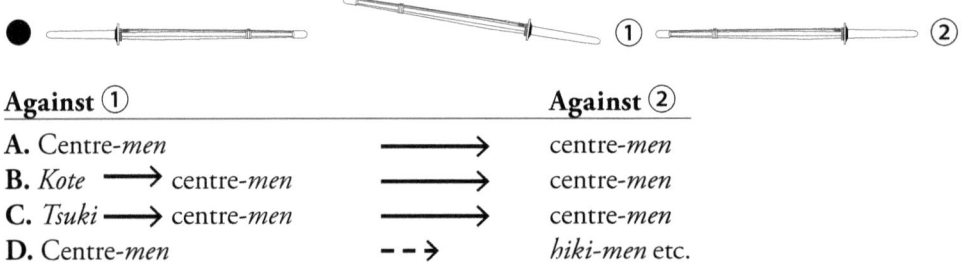

Against ①		Against ②
A. Centre-*men*	⟶	centre-*men*
B. *Kote* ⟶ centre-*men*	⟶	centre-*men*
C. *Tsuki* ⟶ centre-*men*	⟶	centre-*men*
D. Centre-*men*	--→	*hiki-men* etc.

Example 3

With three *motodachi*, the *maai* should be a little further than *issoku-itto-no-maai*, and at the same interval. (In example E, the third strike should be executed while moving back.)

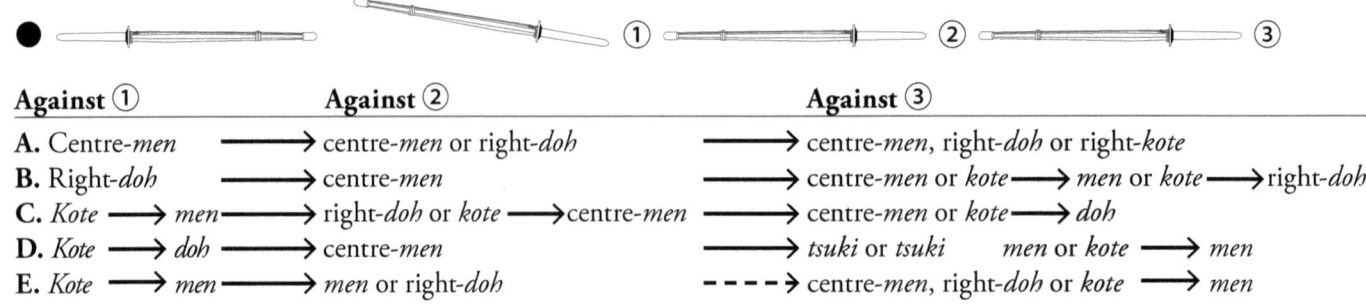

Against ①	Against ②	Against ③
A. Centre-*men*	⟶ centre-*men* or right-*doh*	⟶ centre-*men*, right-*doh* or right-*kote*
B. Right-*doh*	⟶ centre-*men*	⟶ centre-*men* or *kote* ⟶ *men* or *kote* ⟶ right-*doh*
C. *Kote* ⟶ *men*	⟶ right-*doh* or *kote* ⟶ centre-*men*	⟶ centre-*men* or *kote* ⟶ *doh*
D. *Kote* ⟶ *doh*	⟶ centre-*men*	⟶ *tsuki* or *tsuki* *men* or *kote* ⟶ *men*
E. *Kote* ⟶ *men*	⟶ *men* or right-*doh*	--→ centre-*men*, right-*doh* or *kote* ⟶ *men*

Example 4

With three *motodachi*, the distance from ① to ② should be *chikama*, and ② to ③ should be *toma*. Try adding *hiki-waza* and *kaeshi-waza*.

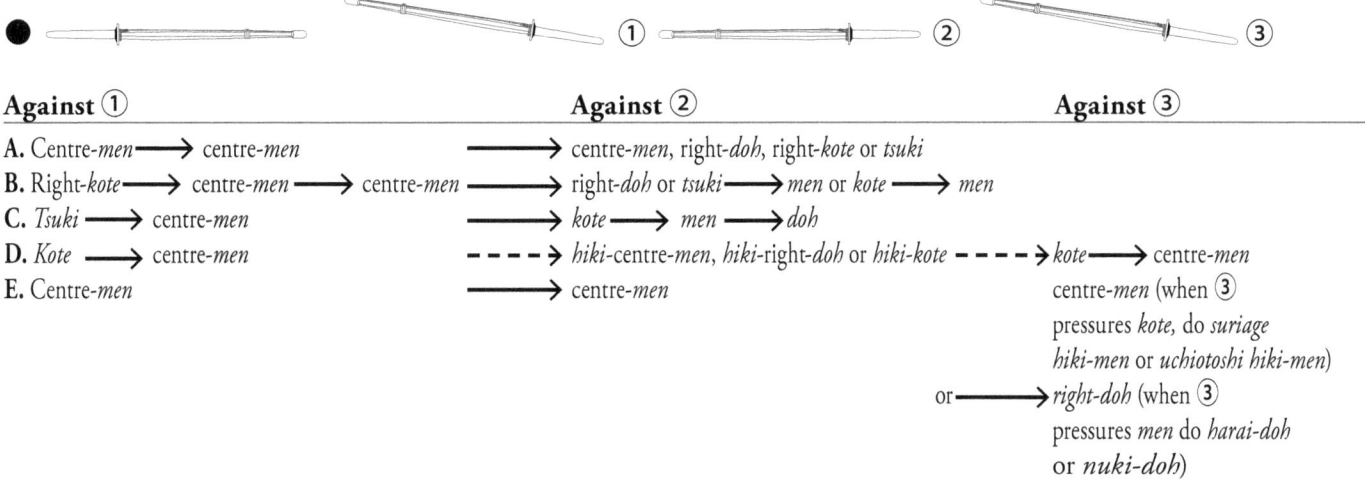

Against ①		Against ②		Against ③
A. Centre-*men* ⟶	centre-*men*	⟶	centre-*men*, right-*doh*, right-*kote* or *tsuki*	
B. Right-*kote* ⟶	centre-*men* ⟶ centre-*men*	⟶	right-*doh* or *tsuki* ⟶ *men* or *kote* ⟶ *men*	
C. *Tsuki* ⟶	centre-*men*	⟶	*kote* ⟶ *men* ⟶ *doh*	
D. *Kote* ⟶	centre-*men*	⤏	*hiki*-centre-*men*, *hiki*-right-*doh* or *hiki*-*kote* ⤏	*kote* ⟶ centre-*men*
E. Centre-*men*		⟶	centre-*men*	centre-*men* (when ③ pressures *kote*, do *suriage* hiki-*men* or *uchiotoshi* hiki-*men*)
			or ⟶	right-*doh* (when ③ pressures *men* do *harai-doh* or *nuki-doh*)

Example 5

Add *taiatari* with three *motodachi*.

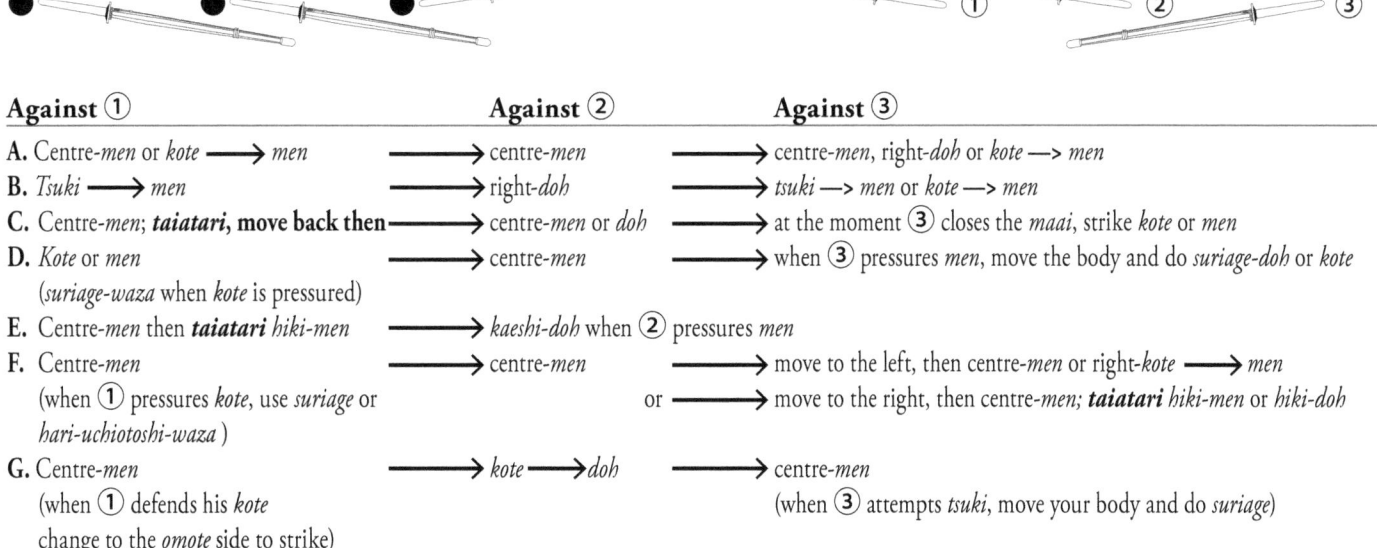

Against ①		Against ②		Against ③
A. Centre-*men* or *kote* ⟶	*men*	⟶ centre-*men*	⟶	centre-*men*, right-*doh* or *kote* ⟶ *men*
B. *Tsuki* ⟶	*men*	⟶ right-*doh*	⟶	*tsuki* ⟶ *men* or *kote* ⟶ *men*
C. Centre-*men*; **taiatari, move back then**	⟶	centre-*men* or *doh*	⟶	at the moment ③ closes the *maai*, strike *kote* or *men*
D. *Kote* or *men* (*suriage-waza* when *kote* is pressured)	⟶	centre-*men*	⟶	when ③ pressures *men*, move the body and do *suriage-doh* or *kote*
E. Centre-*men* then **taiatari** hiki-*men*	⟶	*kaeshi-doh* when ② pressures *men*		
F. Centre-*men* (when ① pressures *kote*, use *suriage* or *hari-uchiotoshi-waza*)	⟶	centre-*men*	⟶ or ⟶	move to the left, then centre-*men* or right-*kote* ⟶ *men*; move to the right, then centre-*men*; **taiatari** hiki-*men* or hiki-*doh*
G. Centre-*men* (when ① defends his *kote* change to the *omote* side to strike)	⟶	*kote* ⟶ *doh*	⟶	centre-*men* (when ③ attempts *tsuki*, move your body and do *suriage*)

Note:

In many of the techniques in example 3, 4 and 5 above, four or five strikes are made. For example, one strike against ①, one against ②, and three against ③. However, it is possible to increase the number of *motodachi* and strike each one only once. Therefore, in the case of Example 4 C, instead of *tsuki* and centre-*men* against ① and then *kote*, *men* and *doh* against ②, at ① *tsuki*, ② centre-*men*, ③ *kote*, ④ *men*, and ⑤ *doh*. Adapt the above examples or create your own methods to practise *sandan-waza*.

6. *Taiatari-waza*—body-checking

When the *maai* is too close, *taiatari* is used to create a suitable distance from which to strike. Also, *taiatari* is employed to break the opponent's posture to create striking opportunities. Furthermore, *taiatari* can be used to dodge an opponent's attack, or bounce off the opponent to create more distance.

From *toma*, pressure the opponent's centreline, advance and strike *men* in a big motion followed immediately by *taiatari* to break the opponent's posture and force them back to the optimal distance to strike again (*uchima*).

Important Points

— Straighten the back and neck, pull in the chin, hold tension in the lower abdomen, relax the shoulders and arms, and strike by inserting the left hip.
— After striking *men*, immediately move the left hand in front of the chest down to navel height, one fist's width to the left of the body's centreline. Conversely, move the right hand down to the right side, and collide with the opponent at hip level.
— The footwork should be resolute. The right foot stops in front of the opponent's left foot, and the left foot just in front of the right foot.
— Prevent the upper body from lurching forward or back in *taiatari*. The centre of gravity is slightly forward.
— Inhale and hold your breath in the lower abdomen. *Taiatari* is done in one breath: strike *men*, *taiatari*, and strike again.
— After *taiatari*, do not strike while still too close to the opponent. Wait for the ideal distance and then strike immediately. Move both hands over the centreline, then forward and diagonally upwards while extending both arms, and strike.
— *Taiatari* from a *kote* strike is difficult. Starting from *men* is the most effective method. Still, learn to do *taiatari* from various *waza*.
— Execute *taiatari* with a vigorous spirit and with the whole body, not just the arms.

Important Points for *Motodachi*

— Straighten the back and neck, pull the chin in, and drop both shoulders.
— Take a deep breath and keep it in the lower abdomen, and take a small step with the right foot while receiving the opponent's *taiatari*.
— Have both hands at the same height as when doing *taiatari*.

A. If the *motodachi* is weak and steps back after *taiatari* following a *men* strike, move forward and strike again.

1. Centre-*men* $\xrightarrow{\text{TAIATARI}}$ (if the opponent lowers the hands and steps back) centre-, left- or right-*men*

2. Centre-*men* $\xrightarrow{\text{TAIATARI}}$ (if the opponent lowers the hands and steps back) *tsuki* → *men*; *right-kote* → *men*; or *left-kote* (or *tsuki*) → *men* → *men*

3. Centre-*men* $\xrightarrow{\text{TAIATARI}}$ (if the opponent lowers the hands and steps back) centre-*men* $\longrightarrow$ (if the opponent raises the hands) right-*doh*; centre-*men* $\longrightarrow$ (if the opponent steps backward and raises the hands) right-*doh*, etc.

4. Centre-*men* →(TAIATARI) (if the opponent raises the hands and steps back) right-*doh*, left-*doh*, right-*kote* or *tsuki*

5. Centre-*men* →(TAIATARI) (if the opponent raises the hands and steps back) right-*kote* → *doh*; *tsuki* → *doh*

6. Centre-*men* →(TAIATARI) (if the opponent raises the hands and steps back) right-*doh* → (if the opponent lowers the hands) centre-*men*; right-*doh* → (if the opponent steps backward and lowers the hands) *men*, etc.

7. Centre-*men* →(TAIATARI) (opponent pushes back or retreats) right-*kote*, *tsuki*, or *men*

8. Centre-*men* →(TAIATARI) (opponent pushes back or retreats) right-*kote* → *men* (or *doh*); *tsuki* → *men* (or *doh*); or *men* → *doh*

9. Centre-*men* →(TAIATARI) (opponent pushes back or retreats) right-*kote* (*tsuki*) → (change to *omote*; if the opponent defends) centre-*men*; right-*kote* (*tsuki*) → (if the opponent steps backward and defends) *men*, etc.

A1: Centre-*men*—*taiatari*—centre-*men* (moving forward)

A4: Centre-*men*—*taiatari*—right-*doh* (moving forward)

B. When the *motodachi* is strong and steps forward after *taiatari* following a *men* strike, use their power to bounce off and strike moving back.

1. Centre-*men* —ᵀᴬᴵᴬᵀᴬᴿᴵ→ (if the opponent lowers the hands and steps forward) centre-, left- or right-*men*

2. Centre-*men* —ᵀᴬᴵᴬᵀᴬᴿᴵ→ (if the opponent lowers the hands and steps forward) centre-*men* → centre-*men*; right-*kote* → *men*

3. Centre-*men* —ᵀᴬᴵᴬᵀᴬᴿᴵ→ (if the opponent lowers the hands and steps forward) centre-*men* —-→ (if the opponent raises the hands) *hiki*-right-*doh*; centre-*men* ⟶ (step forward; if the opponent raises the hands) right-*doh*, etc.

4. Centre-*men* —ᵀᴬᴵᴬᵀᴬᴿᴵ→ (if the opponent raises the hands and steps forward) right-*doh*, left-*doh*, right-*kote*

5. Centre-*men* —ᵀᴬᴵᴬᵀᴬᴿᴵ→ (if the opponent raises the hands and steps forward) right-*kote* → right-*doh*, *doh* → *doh*

6. Centre-*men* —ᵀᴬᴵᴬᵀᴬᴿᴵ→ (if the opponent raises the hands and steps forward) right-*doh* —-→ (if the opponent lowers the hands) centre-*men*, right-*doh* (step forward) ⟶ *men* etc.

7. Centre-*men* —ᵀᴬᴵᴬᵀᴬᴿᴵ→ (if the opponent blocks or steps forward when struck) right-*kote*

8. Centre-*men* —ᵀᴬᴵᴬᵀᴬᴿᴵ→ (if the opponent blocks or steps forward when struck) right-*kote* → *men* (or *doh*); *men* → *doh*

9. Centre-*men* —ᵀᴬᴵᴬᵀᴬᴿᴵ→ (if the opponent blocks or steps forward when struck) right-*kote* (change to *omote*) —-→ (if the opponent defends) centre-*men*; right-*kote* ⟶ (step forward; if the opponent defends) centre-*men*

B1: Centre-*men*—*taiatari*—*hiki-men*

B4: Centre-*men*—*taiatari*—*hiki-doh*

C. When the *motodachi* does not move after *men*—*taiatari*, move to the left or right, or diagonally back left or right, and strike.

Centre-*men*—*taiatari*—move body diagonally back to the left—*hiki-men*

Centre-*men* – *taiatari* – move body back diagonally left – *hiki-doh*

Centre-*men*—*taiatari*—move body diagonally back to the left—*hiki-kote*

Important Points

— The moment *taiatari* is completed, shift left from the left hip, or to the right from the right hip, away from the opponent's centreline while still facing them, and strike.

— When doing 1 to 9 in sections A and B above, try moving the body to the left or right, or diagonally back left or right, and then strike.

D. When the opponent assails, receive *taiatari* like an *ai-uchi* and then strike.

1. If the opponent moves back, advance and strike.
2. If the opponent moves forward strongly, bounce back and strike.
3. If the opponent is strong and stays in the same place or comes forward, move to the left or right and strike.

7. *Tsubazeri-waza (hiki-waza)*

Tsubazeriai is where the *tsuba* of both competitors temporarily come together at stomach height. Take the centreline without breaking posture, and strike while going back the moment an opportunity appears.

Some people misunderstand *tsubazeriai* as a chance for safety or rest. It is also misused to waste time in competitions. This is a distortion of kendo. Correct *tsubazeriai* should be aspired to and mastered.

A. *Tsubazeriai* to *hiki-men*.

1. When stepping back.

1. Take a step back with the left foot while bringing the *tsuba* slightly above the opponent's. Gradually extend both arms forward and when the correct striking distance (*uchima*) is reached, pull the right foot in and strike centre-, left-, or right-*men*.

Tsubazeriai

One step back with the left foot

Pull the right foot back and strike

2. Push the opponent's hands up from below. As the opponent starts to push down in response, make use of their reaction and step back while striking centre-, left- or right-*men*.

3. Push diagonally downwards above the opponent's *tsuba* on the *omote* side. The moment the opponent starts to push up, step back while striking centre- or right-*men*.

4. Step back from the left foot and strike.
    1. Centre-*men* → centre-*men*, left-*men* → centre-*men*
       Right-*men* → centre-*men*, centre-*men* → left-*men*
       Centre-*men* → right-*men*, left-*men* → right-*men*
    2. Right-*kote* (*ura*) → centre-*men* (*omote*), right-*kote* (*ura*) → left-*men* (*omote*)
       (quickly change to *men* if the opponent defends right-*kote*)
    3. Right-*doh* (horizontal *ura*) → centre-*men* (*omote*), *doh* (horizontal *ura*) → left-*men* (*omote*)

Important Points

— It is crucial when striking *hiki-men* to strike decisively and to change the tempo and the type of techniques e.g. small → big, big → small, big → big, small → small, etc.

— *Hiki-waza* should not be done half-heartedly. Preferably it should be a large technique.

— Kick back from the right knee and separate the *maai* with one step.

5. Move back a step from the left foot, and with a small flick of the wrists make the opponent receive the second strike, and then follow immediately with a big third *men* strike.
    1. Centre-*men*, left-*men* (*omote*) → centre-*men* (*ura*) or right-*men* (*ura*)
    2. Right-*men*, right-*men* (*ura*) → centre-*men* (*omote*) or left-*men* (*omote*)

Important Point

— Be careful when changing the small, small → big rhythm. The wrists must be flexible.

A1.1: Stepping back and striking *hiki-men*

A1.4: Strike left-*men*, step back to make a striking distance and strike *hiki-men* from *omote*

2. When moving the body left or right.

1. Take a step back from the left foot, move the *tsuba* over the opponent's, extend the arms and kick the right foot diagonally back to the left or right while striking centre-, left- or right-*men*.

2. Shift to the right and push the opponent's hands diagonally down from *omote*. The moment the opponent responds, move straight back, or back to the diagonal right and strike centre- or right-*men*. Conversely, from *ura* strike centre- or right-*men* in the same way.

3. Step back from the left foot, and strike centre-*men* from *omote* while moving away from the opponent's centreline from the left hip. Then, kick diagonally back to the left with the right foot and strike centre- or right-*men* from *ura*. Conversely, move diagonally back to the right from the right hip and strike centre- or left-*men* from *omote*.

4. Advance to the diagonal right and strike the opponent's left-*men*. When the opponent attempts to receive the strike, move back or forward to the diagonal left, and strike centre- or right-*men*. Alternatively, strike centre- or left-*men* from the opposite side.

5. Move forward to the diagonal right, make two small strikes to the opponent's left-*men*. When the opponent defends, advance or retreat to the diagonal left, and make a big strike to centre- or right-*men*. Alternatively, do the opposite and strike centre- or left-*men*.

6. Step diagonally back to the left, make two small strikes to the opponent's centre-*men*. When they defend, shift diagonally back to the left or right and make a big decisive centre- or right-*men* strike. Also, change by making two small strikes to *kote*.

A2.2: Moving the body left or right and striking *hiki-men*

3. Moving forward.

1. Take a step back with the left foot. While pulling the right foot back, drop the *shinai* tip and take up a striking distance from *omote* keeping parallel to the opponent's centreline. Advance to the diagonal left with the purpose of breaking the opponent's centreline and strike *men*. Conversely, strike from *ura* in the same way.

2. While moving back to the diagonal right, drop the *shinai* tip and shift to an appropriate striking distance from *omote*, keeping parallel to the opponent's centreline. Advance to the diagonal left and strike *men*. Conversely, move back to the diagonal left from *ura* in the same way and then step forward or to the diagonal right, and strike *men*.

B. *Tsubazeriai* to *hiki-doh*.

1. When moving backward.

1. Step back from the left foot. Strike left-*men* without moving the right hand away from the area in front of the opponent's *tsuba*. When the opponent receives the strike, kick back with the right foot and strike *doh*.

2. Push the opponent's *tsuba* down diagonally to the front with the upper body. As they push back, step back and execute a big strike to *doh*.

3. Step back from the left foot and bring the left hand up diagonally forward to the height of the opponent's *men*. When the opponent raises their hands, pull back with the right foot and strike *doh*.

B1.3: Make the opponent raise their left fist diagonally forward and strike *hiki-doh*

2. When moving left or right.

1. Step back from the left foot. Strike left-*men* without moving the right hand away from the area in front of the opponent's *tsuba*. When the opponent receives the strike, retreat to the diagonal left and strike right-*doh*.

2. Advance to the diagonal right and strike centre- or left-*men*. When the opponent defends against the strike, either move back, forward to the diagonal left, or back to the diagonal left and strike right-*doh*. Also, when striking centre- or left-*men*, practise making two small strikes with the wrists and then strike right-*doh*.

3. Push the opponent's hands diagonally down from *omote*. When they raise their hands in response, move diagonally forward or back to the left and strike right-*doh*. It is also possible to do this from *ura*.

4. While moving to the diagonal right, push down on the opponent's hands diagonally from *omote*. The moment they push back either move back, forward to the diagonal right, or back to the diagonal left and strike right-*doh*. This can also be done on the opposite side.

5. Advance to the diagonal left while raising the opponent's left hand. Alternatively, extend the left elbow and retreat to the diagonal left and strike right-*doh*.

B2.2: Move forward to the diagonal left and strike left-*men*. Move back to the diagonal left and strike *hiki-doh*

B2.5: Extend the left elbow and strike *hiki-doh*

3. When moving forward.

1. Take a step back with the right foot. While pulling in the right foot, drop the *shinai* tip and move to an appropriate striking distance from *omote*, keeping parallel to the opponent's centreline. The moment the opponent raises their hands or pressures *men*, step forward or move to the diagonal left or right and strike right-*doh*.

Important Point

— Return to *chudan* if the opponent puts pressure on the centreline. When moving forward or back, it should be done in one movement and with one breath.

2. Retreat to the diagonal left and strike *men*. When the opponent attempts to correct the distance to strike *men* or raises their hands up, step forward and strike right-*doh*.

C2: Move back diagonally left and strike *men*. Create enough distance to strike *men*, move forward and strike right-*doh*

C. *Tsubazeriai* to *hiki-kote* or *hiki-tsuki*

1. When moving backward.

If you move back straight when striking *kote* there is a high possibility that your opponent will strike your *men* or dodge your attack. Pay attention to the following points:

1. Step back with the right foot while pressing down on the opponent's hands, then extend both arms and push forward with the hips. Place the *shinai* parallel to the opponent's, drop the tip as if returning to *chudan* and strike right-*kote* while pulling the right foot back.

2. Strike left-*men* (one or two small strikes) and then strike right-*kote* the moment the opponent defends.

Important Point
— When doing either 1 or 2, it is essential to strike centre-*men* immediately when stepping forward or back.

2. When moving to left or right.

1. Step back with the left foot and strike centre- or left-*men*. When the opponent receives the strike, retreat to the diagonal left and strike right-*kote*.

2. Advance to the diagonal right while striking centre- or left-*men*. When the opponent receives the strike, move back, forward to the diagonal left, or back to the diagonal left and strike right-*kote*.

3. While advancing to the diagonal right, push the opponent's hands from *omote* to the side from above. When they push back, retreat to the diagonal left and strike right-*kote*.

4. Advance to the diagonal right. Push the opponent's hands from *omote*. As they push back change to *ura* and strike their *shinai* (*harai-waza*). It is also possible to employ *suriage-waza* or *hari-waza* to strike right-*kote*.

C2.2: From *omote*, push the opponent's hands and then move the body back to the diagonal left and strike *hiki-kote*

3. When moving forward.

1. Step back with the left foot. Return to *chudan* while pulling the right foot back parallel to the opponent's centreline. The moment the opponent tries to press back or return pressure, step forward and strike right-*kote*. (Quickly strike right-*kote* or *morote-tsuki* while moving forward.)

2. Retreat to the diagonal right and strike left-*men* (or make two small strikes). When the opponent receives the strike, advance to the diagonal left and strike right-*kote*.

8. *Katsugi-waza*

Katsugi-waza* to *kote* or *men

Katsugi-waza can be used when the opponent's *chudan* is weak or is slightly open, or the moment their *kamae* breaks when doing *hiki-waza*. Shoulder the *shinai* to entice the opponent into raising their hands. *Katsugi-waza* is a type of *sasoi-waza* (inviting the opponent to move or attack) and *sutemi-waza* (throwing everything into the attack without fear of being struck).

To execute *katsugi-waza*, take a big step forward with the right foot to the diagonal right while purposefully moving the left hand diagonally forward to bring the *shinai* on the left shoulder. From there, swing the *shinai* down parallel to the opponent's *shinai* while bringing in the left foot, and strike right-*kote* or *men*.

The diagram on the left shows the trajectory that the *shinai* tip takes to execute *katsugi-waza*.

1. From *omote* press the opponent's *shinai* (*osae-waza*) and do *katsugi-men*

2. Raise and then bring the *shinai* down parallel to the opponent's and strike *kote*

3. Change to *ura* from *omote* by dropping the tip of the *shinai* and moving it in a circular movement, then strike *katsugi-kote*

Important Points

— Step out with the right foot and execute a large *katsugi* movement, pull the left foot in and strike in one movement.
— If the opponent's *kamae* is only slightly open, press down lightly on his *shinai* (*osae-waza*) from *omote* before doing *katsugi-waza*, or do *uchiotoshi-waza*. (See 1 above)
— There are two ways to strike with *katsugi-waza*:
  1. Swing up to the diagonal rear, then bring the *shinai* down parallel to the opponent's and strike. (See 2 above)
  2. From *omote*, drop the *shinai* and change to *ura* as if drawing an arc with the tip of the *shinai*, and strike. (See 3 above)
— Strike *kote* or right-*men*. However, if the opponent defends, quickly change to strike centre- or left-*men*.
— If the opponent steps back in response to *katsugi-waza*, continue to strike left-*men*. Carry on if the opponent defends but turn the wrists to strike right-*doh*.

9. Katate-waza—one-handed techniques

Katate-waza is used when the *maai* is far, or if the opponent takes a big step back. It is also useful for overriding the opponent's *seme*, and is also used from *jodan*.

A. *Katate-men*.

Pressuring the opponent's centre, take a step forward with the left foot and swing the *shinai* overhead into the *jodan* position. Step forward and strike right-*men*.

Katate-right-*men*

Katate-right-*men* (different angle)

Important Points

— From *jodan*, raise the upper body slightly to the front and make a spirited strike from your hips.
— Twist the upper body slightly and fully extend the left arm while placing the right fist on the right hip. This keeps your momentum going forward.
— Grip the *shinai* tightly with the little finger of the left hand when striking. Push the *shinai* forward with the right hand as if throwing it towards the opponent's *men*. Maintain the grip with the left hand while moving the right fist from inside the body's centreline to the right hip covering the *doh*.
— If the opponent attacks right-*kote* or *tsuki*, evade (*nuki-waza*) by moving to the left, and strike.
— This technique is effective against opponents who drop their *shinai* tip or open their *kamae* to the right when pressured.

B. *Katate-tsuki.*

Point the *shinai* tip toward the opponent's *tsuki-dare* with the right hand. Execute *tsuki* by extending the left arm and dropping the right hand to the right hip.

Katate-tsuki—left fist in front of the navel

Katate-tsuki—left fist in front of the chest

Katate-tsuki—cutting edge is vertical. Return to *chudan* after *tsuki*

Important Points

Omote-katate-tsuki *Ura-katate-tsuki* *Katate-tsuki* against *jodan*

— In a basic *tsuki* attack, the *shinai* tip, left fist and the navel should all be in a straight line. It is also possible to raise the left fist up to chest height.
— There are three ways to do *tsuki*:
  1. With the cutting edge vertically down.
  2. With the cutting edge diagonally down to the left or right by turning the wrists slightly.
  3. With the left fist in front of the chest and the cutting edge turned diagonally to the right. The moment contact is made with the opponent's *tsuki-dare*, turn the wrist to the right and then return to *chudan*.
— Extend the left arm fully. To stop the body from following, quickly pull the clenched right fist to the right hip. It is important to execute *tsuki* with power in the abdomen and the hips.
— There are several opportunities to do *tsuki*:
  1. The moment the opponent starts to move forward.
  2. The moment the opponent starts to move back.
  3. The moment the opponent stops moving.
  4. The moment the opponent has finished their technique.
— It is important to pull back after executing *tsuki*. As soon as contact is made, pull the right foot back and the left fist back to the *chudan* position.

C. *Jodan-waza*.

Jodan-waza are aggressive techniques which require considerable confidence to pull off. Pressure the opponent from above and immediately seize the opportunity to strike the moment they start to move or strike.

1. *Jodan-men* (*hidari-jodan* - left-*jodan*).

In *jodan-no-kamae*, the left fist and the *tsuka-gashira* function in the same way as the *shinai* tip. First, pressure the opponent's *shinai* tip with the left fist. The moment their *kamae* opens, step in and push the *shinai* towards the opponent's *men* with the right hand while striking with the left hand.

Katate-centre-*men* from *jodan*

Katate-centre-*men* from *jodan* (upper body)

Important Points

— It is important to break the opponent's centre by striking in a straight line from above their *shinai*.
— As you strike down, push your left hand towards the opponent's chest and quickly invade their space.

2. *Kote* from *jodan* (*hidari-jodan* - left-*jodan*).

From *jodan* pressure the opponent's *men*. The moment they try to defend *men* by raising their hands, move forward to the diagonal left and strike *kote*.

Striking *kote* from *katate*-left-*jodan*

Important Points

— When pressuring the opponent's *men*, pull the right foot towards the left then move the right foot forward to the diagonal left and strike.
— Strike with the hips, not just the hands.

3. *Doh* from *jodan* (*hidari-jodan* - left-*jodan*).

It is difficult to strike *doh* with one hand from *jodan*. Pressuring *men*, try striking right-*doh* from *jodan* with both hands (*morote*) the moment the opponent raises their hands to defend.

Also, pressure the opponent's *kote* with both hands, step in with the right foot and strike *men*. Or, pressure *men* and strike right-*kote*. Additionally, the moment the opponent pressures your *tsuki*, *doh* or right-*kote*, practise stepping forward with the right foot as you deflect the opponent's attack (*uchiotoshi-waza*), and then strike *men*.

Striking right-*doh* (*morote*) from *jodan*

D. Practising *katate* techniques.

Striking with both hands is easier, but the technique will not be successful if the left fist is separated more than one fist's width away from the centreline when striking with one hand. Also, it is difficult to strike if the opponent's centreline is not controlled. Furthermore, execute with correct posture and with *ki-ken-tai-itchi*, make use of the whole body. Remember that a valid strike cannot be made without correct *tenouchi*. As you practise *katate-waza*, you will learn how to push and pull with the left hand. Gradually start using the right hand to push the *shinai* into the strike.

1. From *toma* swing the *shinai* overhead in one movement and one breath, and make three strikes to centre-*men*. Complete the third strike as *katate* with either the left or right hand.

2. From *toma* swing the *shinai* overhead and strike centre-*men* followed by *taiatari*. Take a step back and assume *jodan*. Immediately step forward and strike either centre-*men* or right-*kote* with the left or right hand.

3. From *toma* swing the *shinai* overhead and strike centre-*men* followed by *taiatari*. Taking a big step back strike *men* with the left or right hand.

4. After striking *katate* centre-*men* when practising 1, the moment the opponent takes a step back bring the right hand onto the *shinai* and strike centre-*men* with both hands. Alternatively, strike two-handed right-*doh* if the opponent raises their hands. Also, after striking *katate* right-*kote* with the left or right foot forward, bring the right hand back to the *shinai*, step forward and strike centre-*men*.

5. After striking *katate hiki-men* when practising 3, bring the right hand back to the *shinai* and strike centre-*men*, right-*doh* or right-*kote* when the opponent steps forward.

6. Manoeuvre left, right, forward, or back to take control of the opponent's centreline and learn to move freely and strike from any position.

Note:
First, from *chikama* softly grip the *shinai* with the left hand and use the hips to strike centre-*men* from *jodan*. The left hand and right foot should move together (*ki-ken-tai-itchi*).

1. Striking centre-*men* three times. The third strike is made with the left hand (photographs show only the second and third strikes)

2. Strike centre-*men*, *taiatari* then *hiki-men*. Step forward and strike *katate-men*

You can also strike *kote* instead.

3. Strike centre-*men*, *taiatari*, *katate-hiki-men*

10. *Tobikomi-waza*

Tobikomi-waza is used when the *maai* between the opponent is far (*toma*), or when the opponent takes a big step back. It can be used to catch the opponent off-guard and create an opening (*shikake-waza*). It is a type of *sutemi-waza*.

A. *Tobikomi-men*.

From *toma*, catch the opponent off-guard by bending the right knee and pressuring their lower body. Move forward diagonally up as if on tiptoe, making the opponent step back. Lunge forward with the right foot. The left foot should follow immediately as centre-*men* is struck with the arms and legs working together. Furthermore, the moment the opponent bends back, turn to the side and strike *katate*-right-*men* by extending the left arm and pulling in the right hand.

B. *Tobikomi-doh*.

From *toma*, catch the opponent off-guard, bend the right knee and then straighten it (stand on tiptoe) as if pressuring the opponent's *men* from above to make the opponent raise their hands. Immediately jump in with the right foot to strike right-*doh*.

Important Points

— Bend and extend the right knee fully as if trying to jump over an obstacle. The opponent will not expect this sudden movement. Leap in as you extend your arms.
— Jump in boldly and decisively.
— When doing *tobikomi-doh*, face the opponent squarely and strike with the hips with the same feeling as *taiatari*.

Zanshin

Zanshin literally means "remaining heart" and it is an "attitude of the mind", or in Japanese, "*kokoro-gamae*". Even if you strike your opponent, *zanshin* is the state of not letting your guard down but remaining alert and being ready to act depending on the opponent's movements. The idea of the "heart remaining" means that after making a solid strike, you should naturally maintain your strength of mind and your *kamae* should be unyielding. However, deliberately acting in this manner is not real *zanshin*.

The three types of *zanshin* are:
1. When striking, do so with complete conviction.
2. After striking, remain aware of your opponent.
3. After failing to land a strike, remain alert and do not let your guard down.

SECTION 2
Kaeshi-waza

Kaeshi-waza techniques utilise the power of the opponent's attack to enable counterattacking from the opposite side. *Kaeshi-waza* is employed by either avoiding the opponent's *shinai*, or making contact with it. *Kaeshi-waza* that avoid the opponent's *shinai* are referred to as *nuki-waza* and *amashi-waza*. Those that make contact are *uchiotoshi-waza*, *suriage-waza*, *harai-waza*, *osae-waza*, *hari-waza*, *maki-waza*, and *oji-kaeshi-waza*.

1. *Nuki-waza*

Nuki-waza involves dodging the opponent's strike in mid-flight or the moment it has finished, and counterattacking immediately. *Nuki-waza* are advanced techniques that require concentration, precision, and quick-witted movements.

A. *Men-nuki-men*.

1. Moving forward and diagonally up.

Against an opponent who is shorter, the moment they strike *men*, take a little step forward with the right foot and make a small, fast strike in one movement. This should be done like *aiuchi* as you and the opponent strike simultaneously.

2. Moving diagonally forward to the right on the *omote* side.

Move the right foot slightly forward to the diagonal right. As the opponent's strike misses, pull in the left foot and strike.

A2: Avoid by moving forward to the diagonal right and strike right-*men*

3. Take a step back while lifting the body up.

1. Avoid the opponent's *men* strike by taking a big step back with the left foot while lifting the body up. Strike *men* while pulling in the right foot.

2. As the opponent strikes *men*, avoid it by taking a step back with both feet while swinging the *shinai* overhead. Then step in and strike centre- or right-*men*. (This should be executed in the same manner as *choyaku-suburi*).

4. Moving diagonally forward to the left on the *ura* side, or back to the diagonal left.

Avoid the opponent's *men* strike by moving forward to the diagonal left on the *ura* side, or back to the diagonal left while swinging the *shinai* overhead. Strike centre- or right-*men*. Alternatively, after avoiding the strike, hit right-*men* with a left-handed *katate* strike.

A4: Dodge by moving the body forward to the diagonal left and strike right-*men*

B. *Men-nuki-doh*.

1. Moving diagonally forward to the right on the *omote* side.

Avoid the opponent's *men* strike by moving the right foot slightly forward to the diagonal right while striking right-*doh*.

B1: Avoid by moving forward to the diagonal right and strike right-*doh*

2. Moving to the diagonal left on the *ura* side

1. Avoid the opponent's *men* strike by moving the left foot slightly forward to the diagonal left and strike right-*doh*.

2. Avoid the opponent's *men* strike by moving the left foot forward to the diagonal left and strike right-*doh* while bringing the right foot in.

3. Avoid the opponent's *men* strike by moving either the left or right foot forward to the diagonal left and strike left-*doh*.

B2.1: Avoid by moving forward to the diagonal left and strike right-*doh*

B2.3: Avoid by moving to the diagonal left and strike left-*doh* with the left foot forward

C. *Men-nuki-kote*.

Men-nuki-kote is a subtle technique in which it is difficult to measure the correct distance for striking. Bear in mind the danger of being struck as you attempt this, so be ready to follow up with another attack immediately.

1. Moving forward to the diagonal left.

Avoid the opponent's centre-*men* strike from above or below by moving forward to the diagonal left, and strike right-*kote*.

C1: Avoid by moving back to the diagonal left and strike right-*kote*

2. Taking a step back.

Avoid the opponent's *men* strike by taking a big step back. The moment their strike is finished, move left or forward to the diagonal left and strike right-*kote* from above or below. (If the *maai* is a little wide, this becomes *amashi-waza*.)

D. *Kote-nuki-men/kote/tsuki*.

1. Moving diagonally forward.

As the opponent strikes right-*kote*, stand still or step slightly forward to the diagonal left and in one breath avoid their strike and strike *men*. Furthermore, it is possible to avoid the *kote* strike by removing the right hand and executing a left-handed *katate-men* strike.

2. Taking a step back and lifting the hands up.

1. Avoid the opponent's *kote* strike by taking a big step back with the left foot and lifting the hands out of the way. As the right foot is pulled back, strike either centre- or right-*men*.

2. Avoid the opponent's *kote* strike by taking a big step back and swinging the *shinai* overhead. In one continuous movement, step forward and strike either centre- or right-*men*.

D2.2: Avoid the strike by stepping back then forward to strike centre-*men* in one continuous movement

D2.2: Avoid by moving forward to the diagonal left and make a left-handed *katate*-right-*men* strike

3. Avoid the strike by moving forward or back to the diagonal left on the *ura* side, and strike centre- or right-*men*. It is also possible to lower the hands instead of raising them.

D3: Avoid by moving back to the diagonal left and strike right-*kote*

E. *Tsuki-nuki-men*/right-*kote*/*tsuki*.

1. Take a step back and avoid from above.

1. Avoid the opponent's *tsuki* by stepping back and swinging the *shinai* overhead. The moment the opponent's attack is finished, strike *men*.

2. Avoid the opponent's *tsuki* by stepping back and swinging the *shinai* overhead. In one movement, step forward and strike centre- or right-*men*.

2. Moving diagonally forward to the left or right.

Move diagonally forward to the left or right to avoid the opponent's *tsuki*, and follow up immediately by striking centre-, left- or right-*men*, or *tsuki*. In the case of right-*kote*, move diagonally forward or back to the left and strike.

E2: Move forward to the diagonal left and strike centre-*men*

E2: Move forward to the diagonal right and strike centre-*men*

2. *Amashi-waza*

Similar to *nuki-waza*, *amashi-waza* make the opponent strike nothing by lowering the tip of the *shinai* and taking a large step back or diagonally left or right. Then move forward and strike immediately after they have come to a standstill, or as they attempt to make another strike. It is important to carefully judge the interval and keep your distance while maintaining correct posture. A good way to hone your ability to execute *amashi-waza* is to hold your ground as the opponent strikes to become accustomed to the speed and striking style. After becoming proficient at *nuki-waza* and *amashi-waza*, practise with *renzoku-waza* from various cutting angles.

There are eight basic ways to manoeuvre in *kaeshi-waza* techniques as shown in the diagram. Moving forward and back can be done on the *omote* side or *ura* side.

Move back while deflecting the attack with *suriage* and then advance to strike. Or, move to the right while doing *suriage* and then diagonally back to the right to strike. In these examples, strike by manoeuvring freely and precisely while controlling the distance. As far as possible, do not let the opponent's *shinai* get too close, and unify defence and attack in one movement. Strikes must be made in one continuous movement. Defence and offence are completed in unison.

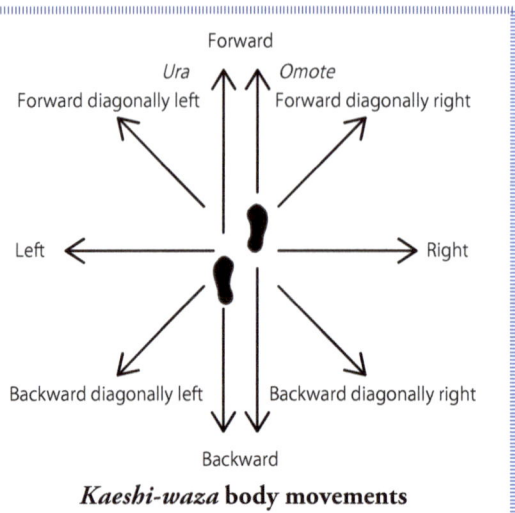

***Kaeshi-waza* body movements**

3. Uchiotoshi-waza

In *uchiotoshi-waza* the opponent's *shinai* is struck down as they strike and followed with a counterattack.

- ● Shows the path of the *shinai*
- ▲ Shows the impact point of *uchiotoshi*

Uchiotoshi-men or *doh* against *men*

Uchiotoshi-waza from the *omote* side

Uchiotoshi-men or *doh* against *men*

Uchiotoshi-men or *kote* against right-*kote*

Omote side or *ura* side against *tsuki*

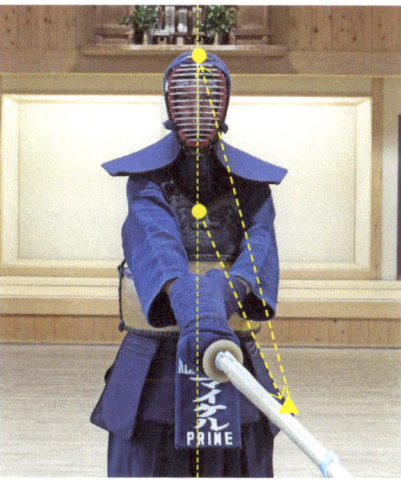
Uchiotoshi-men from the *ura* side against right-*doh*

A. *Uchiotoshi-men* or *doh* against *men*.

1. *Uchiotoshi* from the *omote* side.

If the opponent attempts to strike *men*, it is difficult to strike down if you are not taller. In that case, move to the right side, or diagonally forward or back to the right.

The moment the opponent starts to swing down for *men*, move the right foot to the right, or diagonally forward or back to the right, and strike the *shinai* down. Then, bring the right foot back in and strike *men* or left-*doh*.

A1: *Uchiotoshi-men* against *men* from the *omote* side

Important Points

— Keep to your own centreline while moving away from the direction of the opponent's strike.
— Execute *uchiotoshi* when the opponent starts to bring their *shinai* down to strike.
— *Uchiotoshi* should be done on an angle from the opponent's left shoulder down through to below their right chest area. Use the *shinogi* of the *monouchi* and strike the area between the *nakayui* and the middle of the *shinai*.
— The entire movement should be done in one breath.
— Practise moving to the right or back to the diagonal right as you do *uchiotoshi* followed by a step forward or back while striking *men*.

2. *Uchiotoshi* from the *ura* side.

The moment the opponent strikes centre-*men*, move the left foot to the left, or diagonally forward or back to the left, and do *uchiotoshi*. Strike centre-*men*, right-*men* or right-*doh*.

A2: *Uchiotoshi-men* against centre-*men* from the *ura* side - take a step back to the diagonal left

Important Points

— When striking right-*doh*, swing the *shinai* up as if to strike *men* and then immediately strike right-*doh*.
— It is difficult to execute *uchiotoshi* and then attack right-*kote*. Therefore, do *uchiotoshi*-right-*kote* to suppress the opponent's hands, and then move on to centre-*men* or right-*doh* making a *renzoku-waza* sequence.

B. *Uchiotoshi-men* or *uchiotoshi-tsuki* against *kote*.

1. Do *uchiotoshi* at the front.

As the opponent strikes right-*kote*, immediately move forward and counter with *uchitoshi* directly in front and strike *men* or *tsuki*.

Important Points

— Turn the cutting edge diagonally down to the right. Make a small diagonal *uchiotoshi* action from the opponent's right chest area to above their left hip.
— Step with the right foot and tighten the grip at the same time as *uchiotoshi*.
— Move in parallel to the opponent's centreline. It is also possible to *uchiotoshi* the area around the *tsuba* but instantly move on to strike *men*.
— Keep the grip relaxed and use the hips when striking.

2. Step back and execute *uchiotoshi*.

When the opponent comes in to strike right-*kote*, step back and execute *uchiotoshi* followed immediately with *men*.

B2: Against a right-*kote* strike, pull the right foot back, do *uchiotoshi*, bring in the left foot and strike *men*

Important Points

— Step back with the right foot when executing *uchiotoshi*, then move the left foot in as you strike *men* with *ayumi-ashi*. Maintain a correct interval and do not break posture.
— Take a step back and execute *uchiotoshi*, then immediately advance or step diagonally forward to the left and strike *men*, right-*kote* or *tsuki*.

3. On the *ura* side, move left, up to the diagonal left, or back to do *uchiotoshi*.

Against the opponent's right-*kote* strike, move left on the *ura* side, diagonally forward or back to the left, do *uchiotoshi* followed by *men*, right-*kote* or *tsuki*.

Important Points

— Step to the left from the left foot and do *uchiotoshi*. Move the right foot forward or back behind the left foot and strike. Alternatively, step with the right foot to the right and follow with the left.
 Also, move both feet together and do *uchiotoshi* and then immediately step forward to strike.
— After striking *kote* or *tsuki*, try to move to another technique to make *renzoku-waza*.

C. *Uchiotoshi-men, uchiotoshi-kote* or *uchiotoshi-tsuki* against *tsuki*.

1. Do *uchiotoshi* in the area in front.

When the opponent thrusts to *tsuki*, do *uchiotoshi* in front from either the *omote* or *ura* sides and then strike centre-*men* or left- or right-*doh*.

2. From *omote* or *ura*, move to the side or diagonally left or right to the front or back.

When the opponent's *tsuki* comes in a straight line, quickly move to the *omote* or *ura* sides and do *uchiotoshi*. Then strike *men*, right-*kote* or *tsuki* by moving sufficiently forward or backward, or to the left or right.

C2: Against *tsuki*, from *omote* move diagonally forward to the right, do *uchiotoshi* and strike *men*

D. *Uchiotoshi-men* against right-*doh*.

When the opponent goes to strike right-*doh*, move slightly diagonally forward from the left foot, or back to the left while striking the opponent's *shinai* down to the diagonal right followed by *men*.

Uchiotoshi-men **against right-*doh***

Important Points

— Observe the opponent's right-*doh* attack and do *uchiotoshi* down to the diagonal right. Using the power generated by *uchiotoshi*, swing the *shinai* overhead and strike moving either forward or back while facing the opponent directly.

— Right-*doh* is a technique that comes in from the side. When the opponent starts to bring the *shinai* down, practise striking right-*kote* followed immediately by *men*.

4. *Suriage-waza*

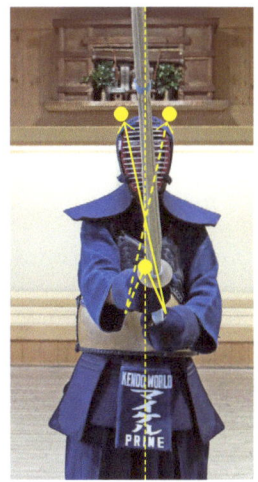
Suriage-waza against *men*

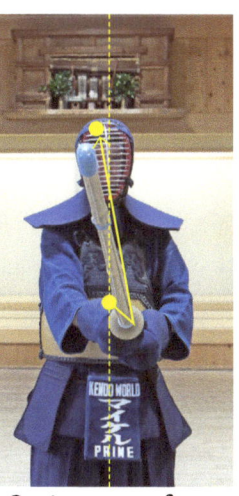
Suriage-waza from the *omote* side against *men*

Suriage-waza from the *ura* side against *men*

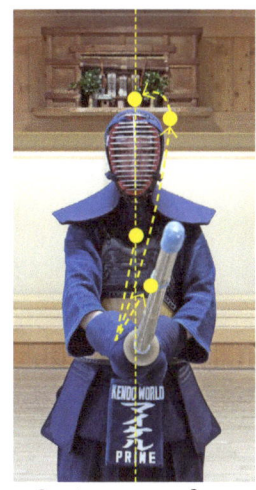
Suriage-waza from the *ura* side against *kote*

Suriage-men against *tsuki*

A. *Suriage-men*, *doh* or right-*kote* against *men*.

1. *Suriage* from the *omote* side.

As the opponent swings their *shinai* down to strike *men*, move either forward, back, to the right or diagonally forward or back to the right, do *suriage* from *omote* and strike *men* or left-*doh*.

A1: Against a *men* strike, on the *omote* side move diagonally forward to the right and strike *suriage-men*

A1: Against a *men* strike, strike *suriage*-left-*doh* from the *omote* side

Important Points

— As the opponent brings their *shinai* down, suppress it with the *shinogi* of the *monouchi* by moving your *shinai* from the left side of their centreline diagonally up to above their right-*men*, and then strike.
— When advancing to do *suriage*, make a sharp movement diagonally forward, *suriage*, and then strike.
— Do not wait for the opponent to attack. Move forward drawing the opponent's *shinai* in and strike.

2. *Suriage* from the *ura* side.

As the opponent swings down to strike *men*, move either forward, back, to the left or diagonally forward or backward to the left. From the *ura* side, do *suriage* and strike *men*, right-*kote* or right-*doh*.

A2: Against a *men* strike, do *suriage-men* on the *ura* side directly in front

A2.1: Against a *men* strike, execute *suriage*-right-*doh* from the *ura* side

Important Points

— Change to the *ura*-side by slightly dropping the tip of the *shinai*. *Suriage* on the right side of the opponent's centreline by raising the *shinai* diagonally above left-*men* but without moving the tip of the *shinai* away from their body.
— To attack right-*kote*, execute *suriage* in a big movement while retreating to the diagonal left, then immediately advance to strike. After striking right-*kote*, try *renzoku-waza* and strike *men* or *doh*.
— There are three ways to pass the opponent when striking right-*doh*:
  1. On the opponent's left side.
  2. Move the right foot forward to strike and then pass on the right side.
  3. Move the left foot forward followed by the right to strike, and pass on the right side.
— Practise moving back to *suriage* and then moving forward left or right to strike, as well as moving left or right to *suriage* and then forward or back to strike.

— Try *renzoku-waza*. For example, after doing *suriage-men*, move to strike *doh*, or *doh* and then *men*. Also, practise moving straight and to the side, up and down, and from *omote* to *ura* to be able to change direction freely
— *Suriage* on the *ura* side, and depending on the reaction of the opponent, change to *omote* to strike, or vice versa.

B. *Suriage-men, suriage*-right-*kote* or *suriage-tsuki* against right-*kote*.

1. *Suriage* from the *ura* side

When the opponent moves to strike right-*kote*, move either forward to the *ura* side, diagonally forward to the left, to the left or diagonally back to the left, execute *suriage* and strike *men*, right-*kote* or *tsuki*.

B1: *Suriage-men* moving forward and up from the *ura* side against right-*kote*

B1: *Suriage-men* advancing diagonally to the left on the *ura* side against right-*kote*

Important Point

— As the opponent swings down to strike *men*, execute *suriage* between the *nakayui* and the area in front of the *tsuba* and strike. *Suriage* as if thrusting toward the opponent's left chest area against right-*kote* or *tsuki*.

C. *Suriage-men, suriage-*right-*kote* or *suriage-tsuki* against *tsuki*.

1. *Suriage* from the *omote* side.

1. As the opponent does *tsuki*, move either forward, back, right, diagonally forward to the right, or diagonally back to the right, and do a *suriage-men* strike from the *omote* side.
2. Against the opponent's *tsuki*, move either forward, right, or diagonally forward to the right from the *omote* side and do *suriage-tsuki*.

C1.1: Against *tsuki*, from the *omote* side move diagonally up to the left and do *suriage-men*

Important Point

— To strike *men*, do *suriage* with the *shinogi* part of the *monouchi* diagonally up to the area above the opponent's right-*men*. For *tsuki*, perform *suriage* to the level of the opponent's right chest area and thrust.

2. *Suriage* from the *ura*-side.

1. As the opponent does *tsuki*, move either forward, back, left, diagonally up to the left, diagonally back to the left and do a *suriage-men* strike from the *ura*-side.
2. Against the opponent's *tsuki*, move either forward, left, or diagonally forward to the left, and do *suriage*-right-*kote* or *suriage-tsuki* from the *ura*-side.

Important Points

— To strike *men*, move the *shinai* from the left side of the opponent's centreline diagonally up to the area above the left-*men*. For *tsuki*, perform *suriage* to the level of the opponent's left chest area and thrust.
— In *suriage-waza* and *kaeshi-waza*, the deflection and striking is done in one movement while moving the body. Strike while moving forward or back.

5. *Harai-waza*

Harai against *men* (*ura*)

Harai against right-*kote* (*ura*)

Harai against *men* (*omote* and *ura*)

Harai centre-*men* against *men* (*omote*)

Harai centre-*men* against *tsuki*

A. *Harai-men*, *doh* or right-*kote* against *men*.

1. *Harai* from the *omote* side.

As the opponent starts to swing down for a *men* strike, move forward, back, right, diagonally up to the right, or diagonally back to the right, *harai* and strike men or left-*doh* from the *omote* side.

A1: Against a centre-*men* strike, from the *omote* side, move diagonally back to the right, *harai*, advance and strike *men* (two movements)

A1: Against a centre-*men* strike, from the *omote* side, *harai*, move diagonally back to the right, advance and strike *men* (one movement)

Important Point

— On the left side of the opponent's centreline, *harai* by moving the *shinai* tip in a semi-circular movement above the opponent's right-*men* without moving it away from the opponent.

2. *Harai* from the *ura* side.

As the opponent starts to swing down for a *men* strike, move either forward, back, left, diagonally up to the left, or diagonally back to the left, *harai* and strike *men*, right-doh or right-kote from the *ura* side.

A2: Against a centre-*men* strike, from the *ura* side, *harai*, move diagonally forward to the left and strike right-*doh*

A2: Move diagonally forward to the right and strike right-*doh*

Important Points

— To *harai*, move the *shinai* tip in a semi-circular motion on the right side of the opponent's centreline above the right-*men*.
— When doing *harai-waza*, think of a flint creating a spark. This means that you should not *harai* and then strike, but rather when you *harai* you should be already striking.
— When doing *harai*-right-*doh* from the *ura* side, it is also possible to move diagonally up to the right.
— Practise the following *harai-waza* methods:
  - *harai* on the *ura* side, change to the *omote* side and strike *men*
  - *harai* on the *omote* side and change to the *ura* side
  - *harai* on the *omote* side, strike *men* and then right-doh
  - *harai* on the *ura* side, strike right-*kote* and then *men*

B. *Harai-men, harai-doh* or *harai-tsuki* against right-*kote*

1. *Harai* from the *ura* side.

As the opponent strikes right-*kote*, move either forward, back, left, diagonally up to the left, or diagonally back to the left, do *harai* and strike *men*, right-*doh*, right-*kote* or *tsuki* from the *ura* side.

B1: Against right-*kote*, *harai*, advance and strike centre-*men* from the *ura* side

Important Points

— To do *harai-men* or *harai*-right-*doh*, *harai* by moving the tip of the *shinai* in a semi-circular motion above the opponent's left-*men* on the right side of the centreline. To do *harai*-right-*kote* or *harai-tsuki*, *harai* by making a small, sharp movement with flexible wrists from the left chest area to the throat.

— Do not just use the hands when doing *harai-waza*. Focus power in the lower abdomen, relax the shoulders, and use the hips.

C. *Harai-men, harai*-right-*kote* or *harai-tsuki* against *tsuki*.

1. *Harai* from the *omote* side.

As the opponent does *tsuki*, move either forward, back, right, diagonally forward to the right, or diagonally back to the right, and do *harai* and strike *men* or *tsuki* from the *omote* side.

Important Point

— *Tsuki* is direct and fast, so it is important to move quickly, keep the wrists flexible, and grip firmly when doing *harai-waza*.

2. *Harai* from the *ura* side.

As the opponent does *tsuki*, move either forward, back, left, diagonally forward to the left, or diagonally back to the left, and do *harai* and strike *men*, right-*kote* or *tsuki* from the *ura* side.

C2: Against *tsuki*, *harai-morote-tsuki* from the *ura* side

C2: Against *tsuki*, move the body diagonally back to the left, *harai*, move forward and strike centre-*men*

Important Point

— *Tsuki* is direct and fast, so move forward or diagonally up to the left, and go from *harai* to *tsuki* in one small movement. Or, move back or diagonally back to the left, *harai*, and advance and *tsuki*, in two movements but one breath.

The *tanden* (abdomen)

Ekiken Kaibara (1630–1714) once said, "The *tanden* is the area around abdomen. It is here that life energy originates." It is the place from which courage and vitality are borne. There is the *shimo-tanden* in the lower abdomen, and the area between the eyebrows is known as the *kami-tanden*.

6. *Osae-waza*

▲ Shows the *osae* points

Osae-men or *tsuki* from *omote* against *tsuki* | *Osae-men* or right-*kote* from *ura* against right-*kote* | *Osae-men* from *omote* against *men* | *Osae-men* or right-*doh* against *men* | Against *men*

A. *Osae-men, osae-doh* or *osae*-right-*kote* against *men*.

1. *Osae* from the *omote* side.

As the opponent strikes *men*, move either diagonally right forward, right, or diagonally back to the right, *osae* from the *omote* side and strike *men* or left- or right-*doh*.

A1: Against *men*, move the body diagonally up to the right, *osae* and strike centre-*men*

Important Points

— *Osae* can be executed with the right hand from above, or by opening the *chudan* stance slightly and moving the left fist as if directing it over the opponent's *shinai*.

— The *shinai* tip should extend towards the opponent's right chest area. *Osae* with the hips in the centre from above without using much power in the arms.

— When striking *doh*, move diagonally forward or back to the right. As the opponent swings down, *osae* diagonally downwards in front while bringing in the left foot. As the opponent starts to push back by raising their hands, immediately strike *doh*.

2. *Osae* from the *ura* side.

As the opponent strikes *men*, move either diagonally forward to the left, left, or diagonally back to the left, *osae* from the *ura* side and strike *men* or *doh*. Right-*kote* is done the same way.

A2: Against *men*, move to the left, *osae*, and do *hiki-men* diagonally to the left

A2: Against *men*, move diagonally forward to the left, pressure *men* from *ura*, and strike right-*doh*

Important Points

— First, shift the right foot to the left, diagonally forward or back to the left, turn the blade diagonally down to the right. As the opponent swings down, *osae* while turning the left hip and bringing the left foot in.
— To strike right-*doh* when the opponent raises their hands in response to the *osae* is easy. However, when the opponent does not raise their hands, move in to attack *men* and strike immediately when they do raise them.
— Striking right-*kote* is known as *osae-kote*. As the opponent swings down, change direction by twisting the hips, take the centre and check the opponent's hands. Also, as the opponent raises their hands, immediately change to a *men* or *doh* strike.

B. *Osae-men*, *osae-doh* or *osae-tsuki* against right-*kote*.

1. *Osae* from the *ura* side.

As the opponent attempts to strike right-*kote*, move either forward, back, left, diagonally forward to the left, diagonally back to the left, and do *osae-men*, *osae-doh*, or *tsuki*.

B1: Against right-*kote*, move diagonally forward to the left and do *osae-men*

Important Points

— To strike *doh*, pressure *men* after doing *osae* and stop just in front. When the opponent raises their hands, immediately strike right-*doh*.

— To do *osae*, turn the blade diagonally down to the right and step forward with the right foot. At the same time, turn the hips and move away from the direction of the opponent. The *shinai* tip should point above the opponent's left hip. *Osae* the area in front of the *tsuba* and bring the left foot in.

— Also, practise going from *osae-kote* to *men*, *tsuki* or *doh*. Also, *osae* on the *ura* side then changing to *omote* and striking *men*.

C. *Osae-men*, *osae*-right-*kote* or *osae-tsuki* against *tsuki*.

1. *Osae* from the *omote* side.

When the opponent does *tsuki*, move either forward, right, diagonally forward to the right, or diagonally back to the right, *osae* and strike *men*, right-*kote*, or *tsuki*.

C1: Against *tsuki*, *osae* from the *omote* side, advance and strike centre-*men*

Important Points

— To do *osae* against *tsuki*, *osae* by stepping to the side of the *shinai* tip.

— When doing *tsuki* or striking right-*kote*, shift back or diagonally back to the right, *osae* and move sufficiently diagonally forward or back to make room to strike.

— To *osae* against a *tsuki* from the *omote* side, strike centre-*men* or right-*men* when the opponent starts to push back, or go from right-*kote* to *men* from the *ura* side.

2. *Osae* from the *omote* side.

When the opponent does *tsuki*, move either forward, left, diagonally forward to the left, or diagonally back to the left, *osae* and strike *men*, right-*kote*, or *tsuki*.

C2: Against *tsuki*, *osae* from the *ura* side, move forward and strike centre-*men*

Important Point

— To do *tsuki*, move back to the left, *osae*, and then advance.

7. Hari-waza

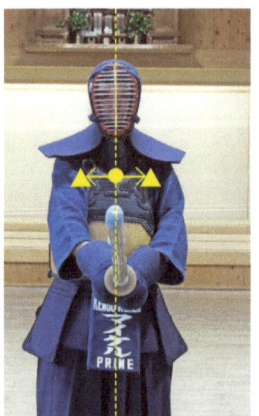

Against right-*kote*, *hari* from the *ura* side and strike *men* or right-*kote* | **Against *men*, *hari* from the *ura* side and strike *men* or right-*kote*** | **Against *men*, *hari* from the *omote* side and strike *men*** | **Against *tsuki*, *hari* from either the *omote* or *ura* sides** | **Against *men*, *hari* from either the *omote* or *ura* sides**

A. *Hari* then *men* or *doh* against *men*.

1. *Hari* from the *omote* side.

As the opponent strikes *men*, move either diagonally forward to the right, right, or diagonally back to the right, *hari* the opponent's *shinai* to "kill" it, then strike *men* or left-*doh*.

A1: Against *men*, move diagonally up to the left, *hari* and strike *men*

A1: *Hari* and strike left-*doh*

Important Points

— *Hari* with the *shinogi* part of the *monouchi*. As the opponent swings down, use the right hand as a fulcrum while shifting the left hand one fist's width away from the centreline from the opponent's left to right shoulder and deflect their *shinai*.

— *Hari* the opponent's *shinai* between the *nakayui* and the *tsuba* using the whole body rather than just the hands.

— After doing *hari-waza*, raise the *shinai* above the opponent's *men*, and bring it down and strike either *men* or left-*doh*.

2. *Hari* from the *ura* side.

As the opponent strikes *men*, move either diagonally up to the left, left, or diagonally back to the left, *hari* the opponent's *shinai* to "kill" it and then strike *men* or right-*doh*.

A2: Against *men*, from *ura* move forward, *hari* and strike centre-*men*   **... or strike right-*doh***

   or

B. *Hari-men, hari-*right*-kote* or *hari-tsuki* against right-*kote*.

1. *Hari* from the *ura* side.

As the opponent strikes right-*kote*, move either forward, back, diagonally forward to the left, left, or diagonally back to the left, *hari* and then strike *men*, right-*kote* or *tsuki*.

Important Point

— As the opponent swings down, using the right fist as a fulcrum move the left hand one fist's width to the right. *Hari* the opponent's *shinai* from their right to left shoulder.

B1: Against right-*kote*, from *ura* move forward, *hari* and strike *men*

B1: Against right-*kote*, from *ura* move to the left, *hari*, then shift diagonally back to the left and strike *men*

Important Point

— To do *hari*, keep the wrists flexible and then tense at the point of impact. Do from the *ura* side slightly diagonally up toward the opponent's left chest area to suppress their *shinai*.

C. *Hari-men, hari-*right*-kote* or *hari-tsuki* against *tsuki*.

1. *Hari* from the *omote* side.

As the opponent does *tsuki*, move the body either forward, back, diagonally forward to the right, right or diagonally back to the right from the *omote* side, *hari* and then strike *men* or *tsuki*.

Important Points

— As the opponent's *tsuki* approaches, suddenly close the grip on the *shinai* and do *hari* with the tip as if to point towards the right chest area.
— Against *tsuki*, move back, right, or diagonally back to the right, and when the centreline is taken instantly advance to do *tsuki*.

2. *Hari* from the *ura* side.

As the opponent does *tsuki*, move either forward, back, left, diagonally forward to the left, or diagonally back to the left from the *ura* side, *hari* and then strike *men*, right-*kote* or *tsuki*.

C2: Against *tsuki*, move left, *hari*, and do *hiki-men* diagonally backward to the left

C2: *Hari* from *ura*, move forward and strike centre-*men*

C2: *Hari* from *ura* and do *katate-tsuki*

Important Points

— With the *shinai* tip pointing towards the left chest area, *hari* with a sharp movement forward and sideways along the side of the *shinai*.
— After moving back, left, or diagonally back to the left, immediately advance and do *tsuki*.

8. *Maki-waza*

   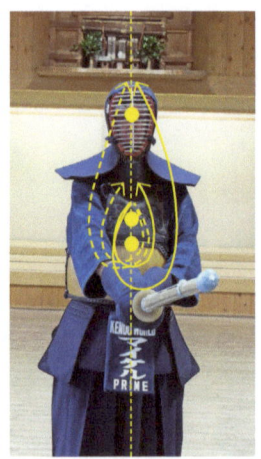 

Against *men* from *omote* or *ura* | **Against *men*, *maki-men* from *omote*** | **Against *men*, *maki-men* from *omote*** | **Against *tsuki* from *omote* or *ura*** | **Against right-*kote*, *maki-men* or *maki-tsuki* from *ura***

A. *Maki-men* or *maki-doh* against *men*.

1. *Maki* from the *omote* side.

The moment the opponent strikes *men*, move back from the *omote* side, diagonally forward to the right, right, or diagonally back to the right, bind (*maki*) the opponent's *shinai* and strike *men* or right-*doh*.

A1: Against *men*, from *omote* do *maki* and strike centre-*men*

A1: *Maki*-right-*doh*

Important Points

— The moment the opponent swings down for *men*, open up slightly to the right, and on the left side of their centreline, move your *shinai* in a circular motion from above the left shoulder, through the navel to the *tsuki-dare* to knock theirs down.
— Do not use only the hands when executing *maki-waza*. Move from the hips, drop the shoulders down, and do not deviate from the centre.

2. *Maki* from the *ura* side.

The moment the opponent goes for *men*, move from the *ura* side diagonally forward to the left, left, or diagonally back to the left, bind (*maki*) the opponent's *shinai* and strike *men* or left-*doh*.

Important Point

— The moment the opponent swings down for *men*, meet their strike by turning your *shinai* slightly diagonally down to the right, and from the right side of their centreline move the *shinai* in a circular motion from above the right shoulder, through the navel to the *tsuki-dare* to knock their *shinai* down.

B. *Maki-men, maki-*right-*kote* or *maki-tsuki* against right-*kote*.

1. *Maki* from the *ura* side.

The moment the opponent attempts to strike right-*kote*, move forward, back, diagonally forward to the left, left, or diagonally back to the left from the *ura* side, bind (*maki*) the opponent's *shinai* and strike *men*, right-*kote* or *tsuki*.

B1: Against right-*kote*, *maki* the opponent's *shinai* while moving diagonally back to the left and strike *hiki-men* in the same direction

Important Point

— To meet the opponent's coming strike, turn your *shinai* slightly diagonally down to the right, receive the strike and move the *shinai* in a circular motion from the right chest area through the navel to the *tsuki-dare* to knock their *shinai* down.

C. *Maki-men, maki-doh* or *maki-tsuki* against *tsuki*.

1. *Maki* from the *omote* side.

The moment the opponent attempts *tsuki*, move forward from the *omote* side, or back, diagonally forward to the right, right, or diagonally back to the right, bind (*maki*) the opponent's *shinai* and then strike *men, doh* or *tsuki*.

C1: Against *tsuki*, move forward from *omote* and do *maki*-centre-*men*

C1: Against *tsuki*, move diagonally forward to the left from *omote* and do *maki*-left-*doh*

Important Points

— Slightly turn the wrists to angle the blade diagonally down to the left. On the left side of the opponent's centreline, and without moving the *shinai* tip away from their body, bind (*maki*) with a small, fast, circular movement.

— When moving back, right, or diagonally back to the right while executing *maki-tsuki*, be sure to consolidate the two movements into one.

2. *Maki* from the *ura* side.

The moment the opponent attempts *tsuki*, move forward from the *ura* side, back, diagonally forward to the left, left or diagonally back to the left, bind (*maki*) the opponent's *shinai* and then strike *men*, right-*kote* or *tsuki*.

C2: Against *tsuki*, move forward from *ura* and do *maki* centre-*men*

Important Points

— Slightly angle the blade diagonally down to the right. On the right side of the opponent's centreline, bind (*maki*) by moving the *shinai* tip in a circular motion with a snap of the wrists while driving forward with the hips.
— Against *tsuki*, move back, left, or diagonally back to the left and execute *maki*.

> ### *Shishin*
> *Shishin* (literally "the mind stopping") is the state in which your mind becomes fixated on only one thing, meaning that you will not be aware of anything else. For example, if you focus on your opponent's *shinai*, you will not notice their movements. It is vital to pay attention to the bigger picture.

9. Oji-kaeshi-waza

Oji-kaeshi-waza is to receive or block (*oji*) the opponent's *shinai* on the *omote* side and then change direction (*kaeshi*) to strike on the *ura* side, or vice versa.

  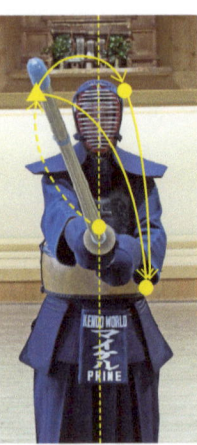 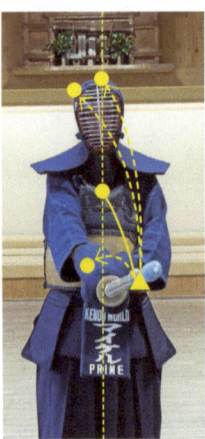  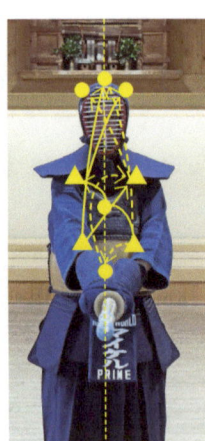

| Against *men*, strike left- or right-*doh* from *omote* or *ura* | Against *men*, do *oji-kaeshi* from *omote* and strike right-diagonal-*men* | Against *men*, do *oji*-left-*doh* from *ura* | Against *tsuki* from *omote* or *ura* | Against right-*kote*, do *oji*-centre-*men* from *ura* | Against *tsuki*, do *oji*-left- or right-*men* or right-*kote* from *omote* or *ura* |

A. Oji-kaeshi-men, oji-kaeshi-doh or oji-kaeshi-right-kote against men.

1. Oji-kaeshi from the omote side.

As the opponent starts to strike *men*, *oji* on the *omote* side, then move either diagonally forward or back to the right or left, change to the *ura* side and strike *men*, *doh* or right-*kote*.

A1: Against *men*, *oji* from *omote*, move the body left, and strike right-*men*

A1: Against *men*, *oji* on the *omote* side and strike right-*doh*

A1: Against *men*, move diagonally forward to the left to receive on the *omote* side and execute *oji-kaeshi* and strike right-*doh*

Important Points

— The moment the opponent attempts *men*, open your *kamae* slightly to the right and receive (*oji*) the strike in front.
— To receive (*oji*) point your *shinai* towards their left eye and place yourself inside an imaginary triangle made from the angle of your *shinai* and body to execute the technique.
— Always take the initiative with *oji-waza*. Meet the opponent's *shinai* with the *shinogi* part of the *monouchi*, quickly turn the wrists and change to the *ura*-side as you strike.

2. *Oji-kaeshi* from the *ura* side

As the opponent starts to strike *men*, receive (*oji*) on the *ura*-side, then move either diagonally forward to the left, or diagonally back to the right or left, change to the *omote*-side and strike *men* or left-*doh*.

▲ Shows the point of *oji*

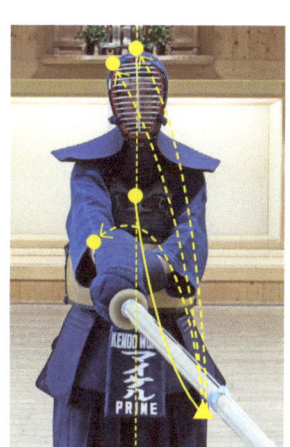

Oji* against right-*doh* from *ura

A2: Against *men*, do *oji-kaeshi* from *ura*, move the body diagonally back to the right and strike *hiki-men*

A2: Against *men*, do *oji-kaeshi* from *ura* and strike left-*doh*

A2: To *oji-kaeshi* from *ura*, move diagonally forward to the left and strike left-*men*

Important Points

— As the opponent swings down, point your *shinai* towards their right eye, and place yourself inside an imaginary triangle made from the angle of your *shinai* and body to execute the technique.
— To execute *oji-kaeshi* and strike *men*, move diagonally back to the right.
— To execute *oji-kaeshi* and strike left-*doh*, move diagonally forward or back to the left or right and strike.
— Keep the wrists flexible to enable a rapid *kaeshi* movement. It is important to be already moving towards the strike as you receive. Do the entire movement in one breath.

B. *Oji-kaeshi-men* or *oji-kaeshi*-right-*kote* against right-*kote*.

1. *Oji-kaeshi* from the *omote* side.

As the opponent starts to strike right-*kote*, receive (*oji*) on the *omote* side, then move either diagonally forward or back to the right or left, change to the *ura* side and strike *men*, *doh* or right-*kote*.

B1: Against right-*kote*, do *oji-kaeshi* by moving diagonally back to the left, and then advance to strike *men*

B1: Against right-*kote*, do *oji-kaeshi* and strike right-*kote*

Important Points

— With flexible wrists, quickly move the *shinai* tip to the right and then strike firmly.
— Take the initiative and execute *oji-kaeshi* and strike in one movement.

2. *Oji-kaeshi* from the *ura* side.

As the opponent starts to strike right-*kote*, receive (*oji*) on the *ura* side, then move diagonally back to the right, change to the *omote* side and strike *men*.

B2: Against right-*kote*, *oji* on the *ura* side, move diagonally forward to the right, change to *omote* and strike *men*

Important Point

— Turn the cutting edge of the *shinai* slightly to the left and receive downwards to the diagonal right. Keep the right knee sprung and kick back to the diagonal right. Change to the *ura*-side and strike *men*.

C. *Oji-kaeshi-men* or *oji-kaeshi-right-kote* against *tsuki*.

1. *Oji-kaeshi* from the *omote* side.

As the opponent attempts *tsuki*, receive (*oji*) on the *omote* side, move either back, left, or diagonally forward or back to the left, change to the *ura* side and strike *men* or right-*kote*.

C1: *Tsuki-oji-kaeshi-men* from the *omote* side

Important Points

— Keep the initiative and will the opponent to execute *tsuki*.
— Slightly open you *kamae*. When the opponent responds by thrusting, use your right hand as a fulcrum and bind their *shinai*. Do not remove the left hand far from the centreline.

2. *Oji-kaeshi* from the *ura* side.

As the opponent attempts *tsuki*, receive (*oji*) on the *ura* side, move either right, or diagonally forward or back to the right, change to the *omote* side and strike *men*.

Important Points

— The change of direction is completed in one breath and the strike is made immediately.
— Practise making another strike (or strikes) (*renzoku-waza*) after executing an *oji-kaeshi-waza* strike.

D. *Oji-kaeshi-men* or *oji-kaeshi*-right-*kote* against *doh*.

1. *Oji-kaeshi* from the *omote* side.

The moment the opponent attacks *doh*, *oji* on the *omote* side and move either left, or diagonally forward or back to the left, and strike *men* or right-*kote*.

D1: Against a right-*doh* strike, do *oji-kaeshi* while moving the body forward diagonally left and strike *men*

D1: *Oji-kaeshi* and strike right-*kote*

Important Point

— Point the *shinai* at the opponent's left hip and open your *kamae* slightly to the right. Using the right fist as a fulcrum, do the *oji-kaeshi* movement diagonally forward. Alternatively, step up to the diagonal left with the left foot, bring the right elbow to the torso, and closing the right armpit raise the left hand one fist's width away from the forehead so that the *shinai* is vertical. Receive the opponent's strike and then counter. Both methods should be studied.

SECTION 3
Jodan-waza

There are two types of *jodan*: left and right. In left-*morote-jodan* (two-handed), step forward from the left foot, and without changing your grip, raise the *shinai* above your head with the feeling of looking down at your opponent. Alternatively, step forward with the right foot into right-*morote-jodan* (two-handed) or right-*katate-jodan* (one-handed).

From *jodan-no-kamae* there is no need to raise the *shinai* as you strike; you only need to cut down. Aim to strike the instant the opponent advances, retreats, or attempts to attack. *Jodan-no-kamae* is known as the *kamae* of "heaven" or "fire" as it is a comparatively aggressive posture.

1. *Katate-waza*

A. Men.

1. Strike the instant the opponent moves forward, retreats, settles, or attempts to strike.

Apply pressure to the opponent's *shinai* tip with the left fist and strike centre-*men*

Important Points

— Take the initiative and constantly look for an opportunity to strike. When an opportunity arises, strike down immediately and decisively.
— Strike as if throwing the *shinai* tip at your opponent's *men*. Twist the right hand to the inside while pushing into the strike with the left hand.
— Do not strike with the arms only. Use the whole body focusing power in the abdomen as you strike.

— When striking, tighten the left grip while pulling the right hand to the right hip with a push/pull motion.
— Keep the left fist on the opponent's centreline and at chest height when striking.
— When facing your opponent, practise striking centre-*men* or moving the body to the right and pulling the right hand down to the right hip.

2. Apply pressure on the opponent and strike centre-*men*.

Use the left fist to pressurise the opponent's *shinai* tip, making them focus on your left-*kote*. Then strike centre-, left- or right-*men*.

Important Points

— There are two methods for striking centre-, left- or right-*men*:
  1. Move the left fist forward and diagonally down the opponent's centreline to pressure their *shinai* tip.
  2. Move the left fist forward and diagonally down to the left to pressure their *shinai* tip or right-*kote*.
— When the *shinai* and cutting edge is held diagonally overhead, move the left fist from the left side to directly above the head so that the *shinai* stands vertically. Quickly move the left fist diagonally downwards, and when the opponent's *kamae* opens, strike centre-*men*.
— Use the left hip and left fist to apply pressure.
— Take a big step forward from the left foot. Quickly pull the right foot up as the left foot stamps the ground.

3. Avoid the opponent's attack to left-*kote* and strike (*nuki-waza*).

When the opponent attempts to strike left-*kote*:
1. Avoid by moving the left fist diagonally up to the left and then strike *men*.
2. Move both hands above the head in a big movement and then strike *men*.

4. When the opponent attempts *tsuki*, defend or dodge and strike *men*.

When the opponent attempts *tsuki*:
1. Lower your *kamae*, do *osae-waza* and strike *men*.
2. Move the right fist away from the inside, hit the *tsuki* down with *harai-waza* and strike *men*.
3. Advance diagonally to the left or to the left side to dodge and then strike *men*.

B. *Kote*.

Pressure the opponent and strike right-*kote*.

1. Pressurise the opponent's *men* with the left fist. As the opponent starts to thrust and their *shinai* comes forward, move forward on a slight angle to the left and strike *kote*.

2. Pressurise the opponent's *shinai* with the left fist. Move the body slightly up to the diagonal left while bringing the *shinai* down to strike right-*kote*.

3. From the *jodan* position where the *shinai* is normally held on an angle, shift the left fist to the centre so that the *shinai* and cutting edge are vertical. When the opponent's *shinai* comes forward, move forward to the diagonal left and strike the opponent's right-*kote*.

4. From *jodan*, pressure the opponent's right-*men* with both fists, turn the wrists and swing the *shinai* down to strike diagonal right-*kote*.

Attacking *kote* from *jodan*

Important Points

— Pull the right foot in close to the left and then step out with the left foot to the diagonal left to strike. (*Nusumu-ashi*)

— When the interval becomes close, adjust the grip of the left hand on the *shinai* and strike.

2. Morote-waza

A. Men.

1. As the opponent starts to move, advance with the right foot and strike *men* with both hands.

2. As the opponent starts to move, retreat from the left foot and strike *men* with both hands.

3. Apply pressure and move as if attacking the opponent's right-*kote*, right-*doh* or right-*men* but stop just before impact and quickly change direction while advancing to strike the opponent's centre- or left-*men* with both hands.

Attacking *men* from *jodan*

B. Kote.

Apply pressure and move as if attacking the opponent's centre- or left-*men*, but stop just before impact and quickly change direction while advancing to strike the opponent's right-*kote*.

C. *Doh.*

Pressurise the opponent's centre- or left-*men* with both hands. Strike *doh* with both hands as they raise theirs.

Attacking *doh* from *jodan*

D. *Uchiotoshi-waza.*

When the opponent pressures your *men*, *kote*, *tsuki* or *doh*, step forward or back, hit their *shinai* down and strike *men* with both hands.

E. *Nuki-waza.*

When the opponent raises their *shinai* or hands when their *men* is pressured, strike *nuki-doh*, or move left or forward to the diagonal left to strike right-*kote* with both hands.

3. *Waza* for use against *jodan* opponents

If your opponent uses *jodan*, the usual way to apply pressure is to point the *shinai* at their left *kote*. If you only use this tactic against a faster opponent, however, you will be beaten. Observing their *shinai*, apply pressure with an aggressive spirit as if you are willing them to attack. Read the direction of the *shinai* tip as they start to bring their *shinai* down and counterattack.

Pressure the left fist, right fist, and throat of a *jodan* opponent. Do not think of protecting yourself.

1. Apply pressure to the opponent's throat. As they attempt to defend by lowering their left fist, strike left-*kote*. Alternatively, if the opponent pulls their left fist back, immediately execute *katate-tsuki*.

2. Pressure the opponent's right fist then quickly change and strike left-*kote*. Alternatively, pressure the left fist and

strike right-*kote*.

3. When the opponent aims for *men*, block the strike and counter with a left- or right-*doh* strike.

4. When the opponent pressures *men*, strike left- or right-*kote*.

5. When the opponent pressures *men*, immediately seize the opportunity and execute *katate-* or *morote-tsuki*.

6. When the opponent attacks right-*kote*, counter with *suriage-men* or *oji-kaeshi-men*.

1. Pressure the opponent's throat and do *katate-tsuki* when they hesitate

1. From a different angle

Chapter 4
Kata

Making the most out of the Nippon Kendo Kata

The Nippon Kendo Kata was created from various styles of swordsmanship when kendo was adopted into mainstream schools and it became necessary to devise a basic, standardised style of *kata*. A committee of sword masters consisting of Takano Sasaburo, Naito Takaharu, Monna Tadashi, Tsuji Shinpei, and Negishi Shingoro investigated representative techniques from different classical schools to create the Nippon Kendo Kata in October 1912. It was revised in September 1917 and then expanded in May 1933, and it is still practised to this day.

Looking at the many changes that kendo has undergone, one can see an evolutionary pattern from practical combat swordsmanship to *kata* swordsmanship, through to the modern sporting version that we practise today with *shinai*. The foundations of *shinai* kendo are found in *kata*, and it still plays a crucial role in the basics. Through studying *kata*, you can learn correct posture and *maai*, and how to strike and move correctly. Furthermore, it helps you understand how serious kendo is, learn breath control, and develop confidence. Despite these positive aspects of *kata*, in recent years *shiai* has been more prominent. This is removed from the true essence of kendo. Many people only practise *kata* in order to pass gradings.

Kata practice is conducted with *bokuto*—wooden swords—for learning the correct cutting angle together with body movement and *tenouchi*. To understand the Nippon Kendo Kata, it is important to connect it to regular training. This can be achieved by practising the Nippon Kendo Kata while wearing *bogu*. When wearing *bogu* and using a *shinai* for *kata*, do it in stages. Pay attention to the differences between the *bokuto* and *shinai*. For example, the *shinai* is not curved and is longer than a *bokuto*. Furthermore, the *maai* when using a *shinai* is different, as is the way in which it is gripped.

In the Nippon Kendo Kata there are seven *odachi* (long sword) and three *kodachi* (short sword) *kata*. In these ten *kata*, the *uchidachi* is in effect the teacher or instructor. *Uchidachi* always initiates the action and creates openings for *shidachi*, the student, to respond to.

The Nippon Kendo Kata

How to perform *rei* when using a *bokuto*.

1. *Ritsurei*.

2. *Sonkyo* and draw the swords so the tips meet.

3. Stand up and take *chudan*.

4. Lower the tips of the swords to the height of the opponent's knees and from the left foot, take five steps backward.

How to perfom *rei* when wearing *bogu*

Do not start from an interval of nine paces as is always the case with a *bokuto*. Instead, start from slightly further than *issoku-itto-no-maai*. Do not take five steps back after standing and taking *chudan*. Strike, and then quickly begin the next movement.

1. *Ritsurei* in the same way as in *shiai-geiko*.

2. *Sonkyo*.

3. Take *chudan* from slightly further than *issoku-itto-no-maai*.

4. *Uchidachi* (r) takes left-*jodan* and *shidachi* (l) right-*jodan*.

1: The *Odachi Kata*.   *Ippon-me* (*kata* no. 1)

1. *Uchidachi* (r) takes left-*jodan* and *shidachi* (l) right-*jodan*.

2. Both *uchidachi* and *shidachi* take three big steps forward from the front foot. When they reach the correct *maai*, *uchidachi* looks for the opportunity and steps forward with the right foot to make a big strike to *shidachi*'s centre-*men*.

3. *Shidachi* takes a step back from the left foot and pulls both hands up to avoid the tip of *uchidachi*'s sword.

4. *Shidachi* then steps forward with the right foot and strikes *uchidachi*'s centre-*men*.

5. When the strike is finished, *uchidachi* takes a half-step back from the left foot with *okuri-ashi*, and *shidachi* lowers the tip of the sword to the centre of *uchidachi*'s face.

6. As *uchidachi* takes another step back, *shidachi* steps forward with the left foot to take left *jodan* and demonstrates *zanshin*.

7. As *uchidachi* takes *chudan* from *gedan*, *shidachi* pulls the left foot back and assumes *chudan*.

Ippon-me (*kata* no. 1) with *bogu*

5. *Shidachi* (l) evades *uchidachi*'s (r) *men* strike by taking a big step back.

6. *Shidachi* takes a big step forward and strikes *men*.

7. *Shidachi* keeps moving forward.

8. *Shidachi* passes *uchidachi*.

9. *Shidachi* and *uchidachi* turn and take *chudan*.

Nihon-me (*kata* no.2)

1. *Uchidachi* and *shidachi* take *chudan*.

2. *Uchidachi* looks for an opportunity and strikes right-*kote*.

3. *Shidachi* avoids the *kote* strike by stepping diagonally back to the left from the left foot and lowers the tip of the sword.

4. *Shidachi* avoids the strike in a semi-circular movement and then steps forward with the right foot at the same time as striking *uchidachi*'s right-*kote*.

5. *Uchidachi* returns to *chudan* with the left foot, and *shidachi* with the right foot while showing *zanshin*.

Nihon-me (kata no.2) with bogu

10. *Uchidachi* (l) and *shidachi* (r) face each other in *chudan*.

11. *Uchidachi* attempts to strike right-*kote*.

12. *Shidachi* avoids the *kote* strike by stepping diagonally back to the left.

13. *Shidachi* takes a step forward and strikes right-*kote*.

14. *Uchidachi* quickly steps back and *shidachi* follows while showing *zanshin* with *tsuki*.

15. *Uchidachi* and *shidachi* take *chudan*.

Sanbon-me (kata no.3)

1. *Uchidachi* and *shidachi* take *gedan* and advance three steps from the right foot.

2. Both come together full of spirit.

3. *Uchidachi* and *shidachi* assume *chudan*.

4. *Uchidachi* points to *shidachi*'s left side, slides the *shinogi* along *shidachi*'s sword while taking a step forward from the right foot, and executes *morote-tsuki* at *shidachi*'s solar-plexus. *Shidachi* steps back from the left foot, turns the wrists to the left and pulls the sword in and with the *shinogi* of the *monouchi*, pushes down on *uchidachi*'s *tsuki*.

5. *Shidachi* then steps forward with the right foot and thrusts at *uchidachi*'s chest. *Uchidachi* pulls the right foot back, and in a circular movement from below and to the left, pushes down on *shidachi*'s sword with the *shinogi* of the *monouchi*, which is pointed at *shidachi*'s throat.

6. *Shidachi* steps forward with the left foot as if doing *tsuki*. *Uchidachi* pulls the left foot back, and in a circular movement from below and to the right, pushes down on *shidachi*'s sword with the *shinogi* of the *monouchi*.

7. From the right foot, *shidachi* takes two quick steps forward and then a smaller third step. The tip of the sword moves up from *uchidachi*'s chest to the centre of their face.

8. *Uchidachi* (from the right foot) and *shidachi* (from the left), return to the starting position while taking *chudan*.

Sanbon-me (*kata* no. 3) with *bogu*

16. *Uchidachi* (l) and *shidachi* (r) assume *gedan*.

17. Both take *chudan* while exerting pressure.

18. *Uchidachi* does *morote-tsuki* towards *shidachi*'s chest, who avoids the *tsuki* by taking a step backward.

19. *Shidachi* immediately thrusts at *uchidachi*'s chest. *Uchidachi* pushes the *tsuki* down to the right while stepping back.

20. Stepping forward with the left foot, *shidachi* thrusts at *uchidachi*'s chest. *Uchidachi* pushes the thrust down to the left while stepping back.

21. *Shidachi* takes three steps forward (right, left, right) and does *morote-tsuki*.

22. After executing *tsuki*, *shidachi* takes a big step back and assumes *chudan*, as does *uchidachi*.

Yonhon-me (kata no. 4)

1. *Uchidachi* moves the left foot forward to take *hasso*, and *shidachi* pulls the right foot back to assume *waki-gamae*.

2. *Uchidachi* and *shidachi* both take three steps forward from the left foot. When the correct *maai* is reached, *uchidachi* looks for an opportunity and both immediately change *kamae* to left-*jodan*.

3. Full of spirit, both step forward with the right foot at the same time attempting to strike centre-*men*—a strike which is not completed.

4. After the strike has been completed, *uchidachi* and *shidachi* take *chudan* as the *shinogi* of their swords grind against each other.

5. *Uchidachi* twists the sword blade to *shidachi*'s right, advances with the right foot and does *morote-tsuki* to *shidachi*'s right lung. *Shidachi* moves the left foot forward diagonally left bringing the right foot behind it while deflecting the incoming thrust (*maki*).

6. When the *maki* movement is finished, *shidachi* strikes centre-*men*.

Yonhon-me (kata no. 4) with bogu

23. *Uchidachi* (l) takes *hasso* and *shidachi* (r) *waki-gamae*.

24. Both *uchidachi* and *shidachi* take *jodan*.

25. Both attempt a centre-*men* strike and then assume *chudan* with the tip of the *shinai* moving along the opponent's centre-line.

26. *Uchidachi* does *morote-tsuki* towards *shidachi*'s chest. *Shidachi* moves the left foot diagonally forward to the left and wraps their *shinai* (*maki-waza*) around *uchidachi*'s.

27. *Shidachi* raises the *shinai* overhead.

28. *Shidachi* strikes centre-*men*.

29. *Uchidachi* takes a big step back to the diagonal left, *shidachi* moves forward and both take *chudan*.

Gohon-me (kata no. 5)

1. *Uchidachi* takes left *jodan*. *Shidachi* takes *chudan* and points the tip of the *bokuto* towards *uchidachi*'s left fist. Both take three steps forward.

2. *Uchidachi* steps forward with the right foot and attempts to strike *shidachi*'s centre-*men*.

3. *Shidachi* steps back with the left foot, and with the *shinogi* on the left-side, does *suriage* to deflect *uchidachi*'s *men* strike.

4. When *suriage* is finished, *shidachi* stamps forward with the right foot and strikes centre-*men*.

5. *Shidachi* strikes centre-*men*.

6. While pulling the right foot back, *shidachi* raises the sword overhead to assume left *jodan* and demonstrate *zanshin*.

7. When *uchidachi* starts to move into *chudan*, *shidachi* pulls the left foot back to also take *chudan*. *Uchidachi* takes three steps back and *shidachi* follows.

Gohon-me (kata no. 5) with bogu

30. *Uchidachi* (l) takes left-*jodan*. *Shidachi* (r) takes *chudan* with the tip of the *shinai* pointing at *uchidachi*'s left fist.

31. *Uchidachi* attempts to strike centre-*men*.

32. *Shidachi* takes a big step backward and executes *suriage*.

33. *Shidachi* strikes centre-*men*.

34. *Shidachi* pushes strongly back with the right foot and takes *chudan*.

Roppon-me (kata no.6)

1. *Uchidachi* takes *chudan*, and *shidachi* gedan.

2. *Uchidachi* and *shidachi* advance. Upon reaching the correct *maai*, *shidachi* starts to raise the sword to take *chudan* and puts pressure on *uchidachi*'s fists.

3. In response, *uchidachi* starts to lower the tip of the sword. The moment the swords are about to touch, *uchidachi* pulls back the right foot and raises the sword overhead to take *jodan*.

4. *Shidachi* immediately takes a big step forward from the right foot in *chudan*. *Uchidachi* pulls the left foot back to take *chudan*.

5. After taking *chudan*, *uchidachi* looks for the opportunity, and attempts to strike right-*kote*.

6. *Shidachi* moves the left foot to the left while moving the *bokuto* in a semi-circular motion to do *suriage* with the right *shinogi*, and then steps forward with the right foot to strike right-*kote*.

7. From the left foot, *uchidachi* takes a big step back to the diagonal left, and pulls the right foot in. *Shidachi* steps forward from the left foot and raises the sword overhead to assume left-*jodan* and demonstrate *zanshin*.

8. Both *uchidachi* and *shidachi* assume *chudan* and then return to the starting position from the right foot.

Roppon-me (kata no. 6) with bogu

35. *Uchidachi* (l) takes *chudan* and *shidachi* (r) *gedan*.

36. From *gedan*, *shidachi* starts to raise the *shinai* tip to pressure *uchidachi*.

37. *Uchidachi* takes a big step back with the right foot to take *jodan*.

38. *Uchidachi* and *shidachi* assume *chudan*.

39. *Uchidachi* attempts to strike right-*kote*.

40. *Shidachi* moves the body to the left, does a small *suriage*, and strikes right-*kote*.

41. *Uchidachi* takes a big step back. To show *zanshin*, *shidachi* moves forward with the tip of the *shinai* pointing towards the throat.

42. *Uchidachi* and *shidachi* take *chudan*.

Nanahon-me (*kata* no. 7)

1. In *chudan*, both *uchidachi* and *shidachi* take three steps forward from the right foot.

2. *Uchidachi* turns the wrists slightly to the right while doing *morote-tsuki* towards *shidachi*'s chest. *Shidachi* steps back with the left foot and turns the wrists slightly to the left while executing a subtle *suriage* with the *shinogi* of the *monouchi*, almost as if supporting *uchidachi*'s sword.

3. *Uchidachi* and *shidachi* take *chudan*.

4. *Uchidachi* steps forward from the left then the right foot while making a centre-*men* strike with the whole body.

5. *Shidachi* moves the right foot diagonally forward to the right, and then steps forward with the left foot. *Shidachi* makes a right-*doh* strike while passing *uchidachi*.

6. *Shidachi* moves past *uchidachi*.

7. *Shidachi* takes a step with the right foot, and moves the left foot forward to the diagonal right in front of the right foot, places the right knee gently on the floor with the toes standing up, the left knee bent at a right-angle, and takes *waki-gamae*.

8. With the right foot as a pivot, *uchidachi* turns the upper body to the left towards *shidachi*, and in a big movement, raises the sword overhead and down into *chudan* so that the tips of the sword meet.

9. *Uchidachi* steps back with the left foot, and both *uchidachi* and *shidachi* take *chudan*. With the tips of the swords touching, both *uchidachi* and *shidachi* move in a circular motion back to the original starting points.

10. *Uchidachi* and *shidachi* finish in *chudan* at the original starting position.

11. *Uchidachi* and *shidachi* sheathe their *bokuto*.

12. *Uchidachi* and *shidachi* return to the starting positions, switch the sword from the left hand to the right, and do *ritsurei*. *Shidachi* then retrieves the *kodachi*.

Nanahon-me (kata no. 7) with bogu

43. *Uchidachi* (l) and *shidachi* (r) face each other in *chudan*.

44. *Uchidachi* thrusts at *shidachi*'s chest. *Shidachi* extends both arms to suppress the *tsuki* technique.

45. *Uchidachi* and *shidachi* take *chudan*.

46. *Uchidachi* steps forward with the left foot followed by the right, and attempts to strike centre-*men*. *Shidachi* steps forward with the right foot.

47. *Shidachi* then strikes right-*doh* while stepping forward with the left foot.

48. *Uchidachi* and *shidachi* pass each other.

49. *Uchidachi* and *shidachi* take *chudan*.

2: The *Kodachi Kata*.

In modern kendo, there is no opportunity to use a *kodachi* unless practising *nito-ryu*. However, it is possible to use the *shinai* with the same feeling as if it was a *kodachi*. *Sanbon-me* (*kata* no.3) is difficult, but you should make efforts to learn techniques like *oji-kaeshi* during practice.

1. *Uchidachi* (r) and *shidachi* (l) place their swords on the left hip after *ritsurei*.

2. *Uchidachi* and *shidachi* advance, squat into *sonkyo*, and draw their swords.

3. *Uchidachi* (*morote*) and *shidachi* (*katate*) stand up and take *chudan*.

4. *Uchidachi* and *shidachi* lower their *kamae*. *Shidachi* lowers the left hand from the hip and points the tip of the *kodachi* slightly away from *uchidachi*'s body, down to the diagonal left.

Kodachi ippon-me (*kodachi kata* no. 1)

1. *Uchidachi* takes *left-jodan* and *shidachi* assumes *chudan han-mi* (*chudan* but one-handed and with the upper body turned slightly to the left).

2. *Uchidachi* and *shidachi* advance, and when the *maai* is entered, *uchidachi* steps forward with the right foot from left-*jodan* and swings the sword down for a centre-*men* strike.

3. *Shidachi* moves the right foot forward to the diagonal right. The left foot follows behind as the body opens to the left and the right hand is raised overhead with the tip of the *kodachi* pointing backward. The strike is deflected downwards with the left *shinogi*, and then a counter strike is made to centre-*men*.

4. *Shidachi* steps back with the left foot and takes *jodan* to show *zanshin*.

5. *Uchidachi* and *shidachi* assume *chudan*, and then move back to the original starting positions.

Kodachi ippon-me (kodachi kata no. 1) with bogu

50. *Uchidachi* (r) takes right *jodan*, and *shidachi* (l) *chudan han-mi*.

51. Both advance until the *maai* is connected.

52. *Uchidachi* steps forward with the right foot while striking at centre-*men*. From the *omote* side, *shidachi* receives and deflects *uchidachi*'s *men* strike.

53. *Shidachi* moves the body forward to the diagonal right, and from *omote*, does *oji-kaeshi-men*.

54. *Shidachi* takes a big step back and assumes *jodan* to demonstrate *zanshin*. *Uchidachi* turns to face *shidachi*.

55. Both take *chudan*.

Kodachi nihon-me (kodachi kata no. 2)

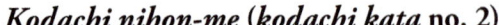

1. *Uchidachi* takes *gedan*, and *shidachi* assumes *chudan han-mi*.

2. When the *maai* is connected, *uchidachi* starts to raise the *bokuto* from *gedan* to *chudan*.

3. At the same time, *shidachi* attempts to suppress *uchidachi*'s sword by moving the *kodachi* slightly down and across. *Uchidachi* then pulls the right foot back and takes *waki-gamae*. *Shidachi* quickly pressures from *chudan* and moves in.

4. *Uchidachi* changes from *waki-gamae* to left-*jodan* by raising the sword.

5. *Uchidachi* steps forward with the right foot and attempts to strike *shidachi*'s centre-*men*. *Shidachi* moves the left foot forward to the diagonal right with the right foot following behind, opens the body to the left, raises the right hand overhead, and with the tip of the *kodachi* pointing to the rear, receives the strike with the right *shinogi* to deflect it downwards.

6. *Shidachi* strikes *men*.

7. To demonstrate *zanshin*, *shidachi* pushes down on both *uchidachi*'s arms to immobilise them, and places the right hand on the right hip with the blade angled down to the right, and the tip pointing toward the throat.

Kodachi nihon-me (kodachi kata no. 2) with bogu

56. *Uchidachi* (r) takes *gedan* and *shidachi* (l) *chudan*.

57. *Uchidachi* starts to raise the *shinai* into *chudan*.

58. *Shidachi* presses down from above, takes a sideways stance, and starts to move in towards *uchidachi*'s hands.

59. *Uchidachi* pulls the right foot back to take *waki-gamae*, and *shidachi* responds by taking a step forward to apply pressure.

60. *Uchidachi* steps forward from the right foot, swings the *shinai* overhead and strikes centre-*men*.

61. *Shidachi* moves the left foot forward after deflecting *uchidachi*'s strike, and counters with centre-*men*.

62. *Uchidachi* and *shidachi* take a big step back into *chudan*.

Kodachi sanbon-me (kodachi kata no. 3)

1. *Uchidachi* takes *chudan* and *shidachi* assumes *gedan hanmi* (one-handed *gedan* with the upper body turned slightly to the left).

2. *Uchidachi* steps right then left, raises the sword above the head from *chudan* into left-*jodan*, and with the next right step, makes a centre-*men* strike. *Shidachi* raises the *kodachi* and executes *suriage*.

3. After *suriage*, *shidachi* then does *suriotoshi* (the opposite of *suriage*) to push the sword to *uchidachi*'s diagonal right.

4. *Uchidachi* immediately steps forward with the left foot and attempts to strike *shidachi*'s right-*doh*. *Shidachi* steps forward with the left foot to the diagonal left, opens the body to the right, and slides the *kodachi* down *uchidachi*'s sword with the left *shinogi*.

5. *Shidachi* slides the *kodachi* up *uchidachi*'s sword to the *tsuba* using the left *shinogi*. *Shidachi* pushes down on the area in front of *uchidachi*'s *tsuba* by extending the arms, and then turns the body sideways.

6. *Uchidachi* pulls back, but *shidachi* maintains the pressure and takes three steps forward. On the third step, *shidachi* puts the right fist on the right hip with the blade of the *kodachi* turned diagonally down to the right, and the tip pointing at *uchidachi*'s throat to show *zanshin*.

7. *Uchidachi* and *shidachi* take *chudan*, and return to the starting position and into *sonkyo*.

8. *Uchidachi* and *shidachi* sheathe their swords. Both return to the starting position, change swords to the right hand, and do *ritsurei*.

Kodachi sanbon-me (kodachi kata no. 3) with bogu

63. *Uchidachi* (r) takes *chudan* and *shidachi* (l) *gedan*.

64. *Uchidachi* attempts a big strike to centre-*men*.

65. *Shidachi* defends with *suriage*.

66. *Shidachi* does *suriotoshi* (the opposite of *suriage*) forward to the diagonal left.

67. *Uchidachi* attempts to strike right-*doh* but *shidachi* blocks the strike and knocks it down.

68. *Uchidachi* moves back and *shidachi* pressures the hands.

69. *Shidachi* strikes centre-*men*.

70. *Shidachi* shows *zanshin* from *jodan*.

71. *Uchidachi* and *shidachi* take *chudan*.

72. *Sonkyo*.

73. Both take three steps back.

74. *Uchidachi* and *shidachi* lower their *shinai* and perform *ritsurei*.

Performing the Nippon Kendo Kata when utilising *bogu* and *shinai* will take about five minutes, even if *uchidachi* and *shidachi* change roles, and it is useful for warming up or cooling down. It will enable you to see the value of *kata* and its relationship to *keiko* in a new way.

Profile

Hirakawa Nobuo
Born in Shizuoka in 1941. Graduated from Tokyo University of Education (now the University of Tsukuba) in 1963 and worked as a high school teacher in Shizuoka while in the budo research department. Retired as a professor from the School of Law at Meiji University in 2011, and has also worked as a lecturer at Tokai University, Kanagawa University, and the International Budo University. Holds the grades of kendo Kyoshi 8-dan and iaido Kyoshi 7-dan. Teaches kendo extensively overseas.

Committee/Federation Memberships:
Former Specialist Subcommittee Member—All Japan Kendo Federation
Organising Committee—World Kendo Championships (4 times)
Instructor and Organiser—Various international seminars
Former Director—All Japan Schools Kendo Federation
Honorary President—Tokyo Schools Kendo Federation
Former Director, Honorary Member—Japanese Academy of Budo
Former Chairman and Advisor—NPO International Goodwill Kendo Club

Competition History:
All Japan Kendo Championships (3 appearances)
Tozai Taiko (2 appearances)
Todofuken (7 appearances)
National Sports Festival (3 appearances)
3rd Place (Individual), Winner (Team ×2)—All Japan Teachers Championships (17 appearances)

Models

Alex Bennett
Alex Bennett was born in Christchurch, New Zealand, in 1970. Received a PhD from Kyoto University (Doctor of Human and Environmental Studies) in 2001 and a second PhD from the University of Canterbury in 2012. Is currently a professor at Kansai University in Osaka. Bennett founded and serves as editor-in-chief of *Kendo World*, the world's only English-language journal dedicated to kendo, and holds the grade of kendo Kyoshi 7-dan.

Michael Ishimatsu-Prime
Born in Ipswich, England, in 1975. Graduated from the University of Sheffield in 2010 with an MA in Japanese Language and Society. Moved to Japan in 2003 and started kendo soon after. Is currently employed as a middle and high school teacher in Yokohama, and has been contributing to Kendo World magazine as a writer, editor, and translator since 2005. Serves as a member of the editorial committee of the Japanese Academy of Budo. Holds the grade of 5-dan in kendo.

www.ingramcontent.com/pod-product-compliance
Lightning Source LLC
Chambersburg PA
CBHW040907020526
44114CB00038B/83